THE 2026 ANNOTATED

MENTAL HEALTH PROVISIONS OF THE

CRIMINAL CODE

Part XX.1

Richard D. Schneider,
Caitlin Pakosh & Lora Patton

UNIVERSITY OF TORONTO PRESS
Toronto Buffalo London

Irwin Law
An imprint of University of Toronto Press
Toronto Buffalo London
utppublishing.com
Printed in Canada

ISBN: 978-1-0498-0497-2 (Paper) | ISBN: 978-1-0498-0498-9 (PDF)
ISBN: 978-1-0498-0499-6 (EPUB)

Library and Archives Canada Cataloguing in Publication

Title: The 2026 annotated mental health provisions of the Criminal Code. Part xx.1 / Richard D. Schneider, Caitlin Pakosh & Lora Patton.

Other titles: Annotated mental health provisions of the criminal code. Part xx.1

Names: Schneider, Richard D. | Pakosh, Caitlin, author | Patton, Lora, author. | Canada. Criminal Code. Part XX.1.

Description: Includes bibliographical references.

Identifiers: Canadiana (print) 20250139839 | Canadiana (ebook) 20250139898 | ISBN 9781049804972 (softcover) | ISBN 9781049804989 (PDF) | ISBN 9781049804996 (EPUB)

Subjects: LCSH: Mentally ill offenders—Legal status, laws, etc.—Canada. | LCSH: Competency to stand trial—Canada. | LCSH: Mental health laws—Ontario.

Classification: LCC KE8841 .S32 2025 | LCC KF9242 .S32 2025 kfmod | DDC 344.7104/4—dc23

Cover design: Kristjan Buckingham

The manufacturer's authorized representative in the European Union for product safety is Mare Nostrum Group B.V., Doelen 72, 4831 GR Breda, The Netherlands. Email: gpsr@mare-nostrum.co.uk

We wish to acknowledge the land on which the University of Toronto Press operates. This land is the traditional territory of the Wendat, the Anishnaabeg, the Haudenosaunee, the Métis, and the Mississaugas of the Credit First Nation.

University of Toronto Press acknowledges the financial support of the Government of Canada, the Canada Council for the Arts, and the Ontario Arts Council, an agency of the Government of Ontario, for its publishing activities.

Canada Council for the Arts
Conseil des Arts du Canada

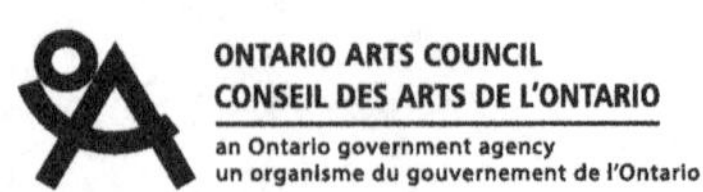

Funded by the Government of Canada
Financé par le gouvernement du Canada
Canada

Table of Contents

The 2026 Annotated Mental Health Provisions of the *Criminal Code* (Part XX.1)

This volume is essentially an excerpt from *Annotated Ontario Mental Health Statutes*,[1] which contains, as well, annotations of Part XX.1 of the *Criminal Code of Canada* dealing with Mental Disorder. The objective is to provide a more manageable volume with particular focus upon the mentally disordered accused. It is intended to be of assistance to Review Board members, parties to Review Board proceedings, and practitioners with accused before the courts or the Review Boards of Canada.

The volume is made up of Part XX.1 along with definitions from section 2 and the statutory provisions regarding defence of mental disorder (section 16) and relevant annotations plus three appendices:

Definitions:

- Section 2
- Section 672.1(1)

Defence of Mental Disorder: Section 16

Part XX.1: Mental Disorder in the *Criminal Code*—The Annotated Statute

- Assessment Orders
- Assessment Reports
- Protected Statements
- Fitness to Stand Trial
- Verdict of Not Criminally Responsible on Account of Mental Disorder
- Review Boards
- Disposition Hearings
- Dispositions by a Court or Review Board
- Terms of Dispositions
- High-Risk Accused
- Dual Status Offenders
- Appeals
- Review of Dispositions
- Power to Compel Appearance
- Stay of Proceedings
- Interprovincial Transfers
- Enforcement of Orders and Regulations

Appendix A: Fitness to Stand Trial and Criminal Responsibility: An Introductory Overview

1 R.D. Schneider, C. Pakosh & L. Patton, *Annotated Ontario Mental Health Statutes*, 5e (Toronto: Irwin Law, 2022).

Appendix B: Review Board Rules of Procedure

Appendix C: *Criminal Code* Forms

- Form 48: Assessment Order of the Court
- Form 48.1: Assessment Order of the Review Board
- Treatment Order (section 672.58)
- "Keep Fit" Order (section 672.29)
- Hospital Pending Review Board (section 672.46(2))
- Disposition: Detention in Hospital (section 672.54(c))
- Disposition: Discharge Subject to Conditions (section 672.54(b))
- Form 6: Hospital Assessment: Out of Custody
- Form 8: Hospital Assessment: In Custody

PART XX.1

***Criminal Code*, R.S.C. 1985, c. C-46, as amended by R.S., c. C-46, Part XXVIII; R.S., 1985, c. 27 (1st Supp.), ss. 101(E), 184, 203, c. 1 (4th Supp.), ss. 17, 18(F), c. 42 (4th Supp.), ss. 6–8; 1991, c. 43, s. 8; 1992, c. 1, s. 58; 1993, c. 45, ss. 12–14; 1994, c. 44, s. 84; 1995, c. 22, ss. 9, 10, 18; 1997, c. 18, s. 115, c. 30, s. 3, c. 39, s. 3; 1998, c. 37, s. 24; 1999, c. 3, s. 58, c. 5, ss. 45–47, c. 25, ss. 24–27 (Preamble); 2000, c. 10, s. 24; 2002, c. 1, ss. 185, 186, c. 13, ss. 85, 86(F).**

Definitions: from Section 2

"mental disorder" means a disease of the mind (*troubles mentaux*);

CASELAW

***R. v. Cooper* (1979), [1980] 1 S.C.R. 1149**— *"Mental disorder"* is defined as "disease of the mind." Disease of the mind "embraces any illness, disorder or abnormal condition which impairs the human mind and its functioning." The definition from the perspective of criminal law is broad. Mental disorder is a necessary, but not sufficient, condition for one to be found unfit to stand trial.

* * * * *

"unfit to stand trial" means unable on account of mental disorder to conduct a defence at any stage of the proceedings before a verdict is rendered or to instruct counsel to do so, and, in particular, unable on account of mental disorder to

(a) understand the nature or object of the proceedings,
(b) understand the possible consequences of the proceedings, or
(c) communicate with counsel.

Commentary: Over the years there has been much controversy within and among the judiciary, among academics, within the bar, and among the psychiatric forensic experts called to give evidence with respect to the so-called *Taylor* test. *Taylor*, below, has been the source of much debate and confusion over the years; said *inter alia* to be internally inconsistent, said to set the bar too low, said to start off with three fitness criteria (section 2) yet conclude with one singular test.

However, recently, the Ontario Court of Appeal released its decision in *R. v. Bharwani*,[2] which rewrites *Taylor* in a way that comports much more closely with how the various practitioners and

2 *R. v. Bharwani*, 2023 ONCA 203.

stakeholders felt the test should operate. A five-judge panel of the Court of Appeal revisited the substance of the test for "unfit to stand trial."[3]

While the Court in *Bharwani* did not overturn *Taylor*, it did explain how *Taylor* should be interpreted. It is clear that there is one test to be considered: "the fitness test."[4]

The starting point in considering unfitness to stand trial is, as set out above, section 2 of the *Criminal Code*.

This definition is said to be merely a codification of the existing common law. The three "in particulars" are now with *Bharwani* clarified to be "touchstones" along with the other *Taylor* test questions[5] that may be considered in informing the fundamental question as to whether or not an accused is *unable on account of mental disorder to—before a verdict is rendered—conduct a defence at any stage of the proceedings* or *instruct counsel to do so*.

As set out in the excerpts below, to be fit, the accused must be capable of communicating rationally with counsel or the court. The accused must have a reality-based understanding of their legal situation, be able to maintain a meaningful presence, and have the capacity to meaningfully participate in the trial process. These are touchstones for the fitness inquiry and the determination of the fundamental question of whether the accused can fairly participate.

Very importantly, the Court underlines that while there is one singular test—"the fitness test," it has to be applied in a contextualized manner. So, as has been suggested in the past, two quite different clinical entities may be deemed "fit to stand trial" as a function of their quite different legal predicaments, timelines, degrees of participation required, complexity, etc. Elasticity is an inherent part of the contextualized analysis. A nuanced approach must be taken.

From the perspective of a legal practitioner in the courtroom, the most significant aspects of the *Bharwani* case are set out in the paragraphs below:

> [107] To summarize, properly interpreted, *Taylor* stands for the following propositions:
>
> 1. The s. 2 definition of "unfit to stand trial"—which at its core concerns itself with whether the accused is unable on account of mental disorder to conduct a defence or instruct counsel to do so—is the test for determining fitness. While it is open to the court to interpret that test in accordance with the principles of statutory interpretation, it is not open to the court to ignore the statutory test and create a new one.
> 2. As the s. 2 definition is a statutory entrenchment of the prior case law in the area, that case law guides the interpretation of its content. Based on that case law, an accused must be capable of communicating "rationally" with counsel or the court in order to be fit. This includes an inquiry into whether an accused is able to understand relevant information, apply that information in the context of their decision-making, and intelligibly communicate.
> 3. The touchstones of the s. 2 fitness inquiry—whether the accused can be meaningfully present and meaningfully participate at their trial—inform a purposive interpretation and application of the s. 2 fitness test. They do not constitute a stand-alone test for fitness.
> 4. The accused need not have the capacity to engage in analytic thinking in the sense that the accused need not be capable of making decisions in their own best interests.[6]

3 *Ibid.*

4 The test is actually the "unfitness to stand trial test" in that we are all presumed to be "fit"; the test pertains to those who may not be (s. 2).

5 This has always been a mischaracterization/misnomer. These questions came from an old Law Reform Commission of Canada study report as questions that could be of assistance in informing a decision as to one's unfitness.

6 While it is true that what is in "one's own best interests" is a matter of perspective, one might argue that where an objective failure to act in one's own best interests is the product of a mental disorder that has rendered the accused incapable of rational thought, the "rules" should step in to protect.

> . . .
>
> [110] Some have suggested that the fitness test from *Taylor* can simply be applied by obtaining answers to the *Taylor* test questions.
>
> [111] Let us pause here to observe that the label "*Taylor* test questions" is a bit of a mystery. The questions, as previously set out in these reasons, are of uncertain origin. However, one thing is for certain: they are not to be found in the *Taylor* decision.
>
> [112] In any event, for the reasons previously given, we agree with all counsel on appeal that those questions should never be used as the definitive test for fitness. While the questions are undoubtedly helpful in providing insight into an accused's fitness, they will often fall short of the mark in terms of exploring whether an accused is unfit to stand trial because unfitness, as a state and as a legal standard, is far more complex. Quite simply, as already shown, determining an accused's fitness to stand trial demands a much more nuanced inquiry than simply placing tick marks beside seven questions that can be answered "correctly".
>
> . . .
>
> [167] To sum up, the following principles should inform all fitness assessments:
>
> 1. There is one fitness test for all accused, whether represented by counsel or not. This test is applied contextually.
> 2. The test for fitness is set out in the statutory definition of "unfit to stand trial" in s. 2 of the *Criminal Code.*
> 3. A person is unfit to stand trial if, on account of mental disorder, the person is unable to conduct a defence or to instruct counsel to do so.
> 4. The purpose of the s. 2 fitness test is to ensure that the accused can be meaningfully present and meaningfully participate at their trial. These touchstones inform a purposive interpretation and application of the s. 2 fitness test and do not themselves constitute a stand-alone test.
> 5. The *Taylor* test questions are not a sufficient surrogate for assessing fitness but are helpful in providing insights into an accused's abilities in relation to the s. 2 criteria. Applying the fitness test is more nuanced than the questions recognize.
> 6. The accused must have a reality-based understanding of the nature and object and possible consequences of the proceedings.
> 7. The accused must have the ability to make decisions. This involves the ability to understand available options, the ability to select from those options, the ability to understand the basic consequences arising from those options, and the ability to intelligibly communicate to either counsel or the court the decision arrived upon.
> 8. The accused need not have the capacity to engage in analytic thinking in the sense that the accused need not be capable of making decisions in their own best interests.

More recently, in July 2025, the Supreme Court of Canda reviewed and upheld the decision of the Ontario Court of Appeal in *Bharwani*. The Court concluded that an accused is fit to stand trial when they are able to make and communicate reality-based decisions in the conduct of their defence or instruct counsel to do so:

> To conclude, the text, statutory context, and purpose of the definition of "unfit to stand trial" support an interpretation of the capacity threshold that requires an accused to be able to make reality-based decisions in the conduct of their defence and intelligibly communicate these decisions to counsel or the court. This necessitates a reality-based understanding of the nature or object of and possible consequences of the proceedings, as well as an ability to understand the available options

> and their consequences, and to select between those options when making decisions. The accused is not required to make decisions that are in their best interests, but cannot be overwhelmed by delusions, hallucinations, or other symptoms of their mental disorder when making and communicating these decisions. [at para. 77, emphases added]

> ... The primary consideration is always assessing the extent to which an accused's mental disorder impairs their understanding of reality when making decisions in their defence. [at para. 78]

> This level of capacity falls short of requiring effective or wise decisions. That an accused may make objectively poor decisions in the conduct of their defence is irrelevant to the issue of their fitness to stand trial. [at para. 81, emphasis added]

The Court went on to say that the same standard of fitness applies to all accused, whether represented or not (the Court of Appeal indicated that the absence or presence of counsel may be relevant to that contextual assessment). Borrowing from the Court of Appeal's earlier decision, the ability to conduct a defence in this context encompasses: 1) the right to challenge the Crown's case, 2) the right to advance a defence, and 3) the right to address the trier of fact. To be fit, an accused must also be able to receive disclosure and understand the concept of disclosure. And, depending upon the legal context, an accused must not only have the capacity to communicate about ordinary matters; the accused must "comprehend the details of the evidence, which in a case of this nature must constitute a minute investigation" (Pritchard, p. 135).

* * * * *

CASELAW

THE FITNESS TEST

***R. v. Bharwani,* 2025 SCC 26** – The "heart" of the fitness test is whether the accused's mental condition renders them unable to conduct a defence. The accused must be able to make reality-based decisions in the conduct of their defence or instruct counsel to do so.

> To conclude, the text, statutory context, and purpose of the definition of "unfit to stand trial" support an interpretation of the capacity threshold that requires an accused to be able to make reality-based decisions in the conduct of their defence and intelligibly communicate these decisions to counsel or the court. This necessitates a reality-based understanding of the nature or object of and possible consequences of the proceedings, as well as an ability to understand the available options and their consequences, and to select between those options when making decisions. The accused is not required to make decisions that are in their best interests, but cannot be overwhelmed by delusions, hallucinations, or other symptoms of their mental disorder when making and communicating these decisions. [at para. 77, emphases added]

> ... The primary consideration is always assessing the extent to which an accused's mental disorder impairs their understanding of reality when making decisions in their defence [at para. 78],

> This level of capacity falls short of requiring effective or wise decisions. That an accused may make objectively poor decisions in the conduct of their defence is irrelevant to the issue of their fitness to stand trial [at para. 81, emphasis added],

The Court went on to say that the same standard of fitness applies to all accused, whether represented or not (the Court of Appeal indicated that the absence or presence of counsel may be relevant to that assessment). Borrowing from the Court of Appeal's earlier decision, the ability to conduct a defence in this context encompasses: 1) the right to challenge the Crown's case, 2) the right to advance a defence, and 3) the right to address the trier of fact. To be fit, an accused must also be able to receive disclosure and understand the concept of disclosure. And, depending upon the legal context, an accused must not only have the capacity to communicate about ordinary matters; the accused must "comprehend the details of the evidence, which in a case of this nature must constitute a minute investigation" (Pritchard, p. 135).

***Clayton (Re)*, 2025 ONCA 305** — The Court or Review Board, in applying the fitness test, must do so "contextually" as set out by the Court of Appeal in Bharwani. Specifically, the Court or Review Board must consider the accused's specific legal predicament or specific legal context. It may be, for example, that an accused is deemed "fit" in respect of one charge but unfit in respect of other more complicated charges that will require more engagement over a longer period of time.

***R. v. Bharwani*, 2023 ONCA 203** — The fitness to stand trial test is set out in section 2 of the *Criminal Code* under "unfit to stand trial." That definition sets out that a person is unfit if, on account of mental disorder, the person is unable to conduct a defence or to instruct counsel to do so. The test is applied contextually and with nuance. The purpose of the test is to ensure that the accused can be meaningfully present and meaningfully participate in their trial. *Taylor* test questions provide helpful insights into an accused's ability in relation to the section 2 criteria but are "not a sufficient surrogate for assessing fitness."[7] The accused must have a reality-based understanding of the nature, object, and possible consequences of the proceedings and they must have the ability to make decisions, though the accused does not need to have the capacity to engage in analytic thinking in that the accused does not need to be capable to act in their own best interests.

***R. v. Taylor*, [1992] O.J. No. 2394 (C.A.)** — The fitness to stand trial test is the "limited cognitive capacity test." The test to be applied is one of limited cognitive capacity, whether the accused understands the nature and object of the proceedings, understands the possible consequences, and can recount to counsel the necessary facts relating to the offence in such a way that counsel can then properly present a defence. It is not necessary that the accused be able to meet some higher test of analytic capacity or capacity to make rational decisions beneficial to himself.[8] **[Note:** *Taylor* is now "explained" in *Bharwani*, above. It is important that caselaw that refers to or imports *Taylor* now be reread through the *Bharwani* lens.]

***R. v. Adam*, 2013 ONSC 373** — Despite suffering from a mental disorder, the fitness inquiry demands that the accused person receive a fair trial. In this context, *meaningful* participation is required. For an accused person in a criminal trial, *meaningful* participation can only mean the ability to defend oneself. The three arms of the fitness test in section 2(a) to (c) are not free-standing criteria to be mechanically applied. On a more fundamental level, public confidence in the administration of justice may be shaken and undermined by the *appearance* of unfairness, which could arise if the accused's troubling conduct or behaviour — a result of their debilitating mental illness — is repeated at trial in front of a jury, quickly degenerating the proceedings into a cruel spectacle that would irretrievably tarnish the appearance of justice.

***R. v. Morrissey*, 2007 ONCA 770, leave to appeal to S.C.C. refused [2008] S.C.C.A. No. 102** — Testimonial competence is not a condition precedent to fitness to stand trial. The third branch of the fitness test — the ability to communicate with counsel — does not encompass the standard that the accused be competent to testify and specifically, that the accused be competent to testify

7 *R. v. Bharwani*, above note 2 at para. 167.

8 Note, however, that amnesia or an inability to recall the events in question is not a basis for unfitness.

about the critical events of the offence and to relate them to their lawyer.[9] At para. 40: "amnesia has never been considered, by itself, to be a basis for declaring the accused unfit for trial or for relief from prosecution or conviction."

***R. v. Whittle*, [1994] 2 S.C.R. 914**—The *Taylor* test was adopted by the Supreme Court of Canada. In this case, the schizophrenic accused was arrested for failure to pay fines. While in custody, he expressed a desire to speak to police about a murder and three robberies. Appropriate right to counsel were provided by attending officers. The accused waived his right to silence and wanted to speak to police about the crimes to stop the voices in his head. The Supreme Court of Canada found that the statements were voluntary and admissible. The accused understood what he was saying, he understood the court process, and was fit to instruct counsel. As a result of the voices telling the accused to unburden himself, he simply did not care about the consequences. The Supreme Court of Canada confirmed that the accused does not need to act in his own best interests.[10]

***R. v. Steele* (1991), 63 C.C.C. (3d) 149 (Que. C.A.)** — An accused is incapable of conducting their defence if they cannot distinguish between available pleas; does not understand the nature or purpose of the proceedings, including the respective roles of the judge, jury, and counsel; is unable to communicate with counsel rationally or make critical decisions on counsel's advice; or is unable to take the stand to testify, if necessary.

APPLICATION—IN GENERAL

***R. v. Jaser*, 2015 ONSC 4729**—The accused's disruption of the trial process by misbehaving or engaging in outbursts, by having difficulty in maintaining a collaborative relationship with his counsel, and by having an inability to understand and abide by the rulings of the court all raise concerns related to the expeditious conduct of the trial, but these concerns do not affect the application of the proper test to determine if the accused is capable of communicating with counsel for the purpose of conducting their defence.[11]

***R. v. Hureau*, 2014 YKSC 48** — The Crown's *certiorari* application to quash a portion of the trial judge's decision was granted. The trial judge found that the accused was fit to instruct counsel *and* that the accused was not fit to conduct a defence on his own. The *Criminal Code* provides for only two possible verdicts on a fitness hearing: fit to stand trial or unfit to stand trial. One of the findings pronounced by the trial judge—that the accused is fit to stand trial if represented by counsel—is not contemplated by the *Criminal Code*. The trial judge therefore exceeded the court's jurisdiction. The trial judge's other finding—that the accused is unfit to stand trial on the basis he was unable to conduct a defence on his own—is a valid verdict within that court's jurisdiction.

***R. v. B. (B.)*, [2009] O.J. No. 863 (S.C.J.)**—Where the expert opinion is that the accused is choosing not to answer questions regarding the trial process and is generally uncooperative with counsel, and while there is no indication of a mental disorder, the threshold for ordering a fitness assessment has not been met.[12]

9 *R. v. Morrissey*, 2007 ONCA 770 at para. 26.

10 Note that while the Supreme Court of Canada found that the threshold or standard for competency should be the same at all junctures and imported the *Taylor* standard into its consideration of competency to make a statement, there has been no fulsome consideration of the fitness test by the Supreme Court of Canada post-*Taylor*.

11 *R. v. Jaser*, 2015 ONSC 4729 at para. 43, citing *R. v. Taylor*, [1992] O.J. No. 2394 at para. 568 (C.A.).

12 Content reproduced with permission from R.D. Schneider & H. Bloom, *Fitness to Stand Trial: Fairness First & Foremost* (Toronto: Irwin Law, 2018) at Appendix A, 201 [*Fitness to Stand Trial*].

***R. v. King*, 2007 ONCA 713, leave to appeal to the S.C.C. dismissed [2008] S.C.C.A. No. 133**—The accused sees himself as having no role to play in the proceedings because he disavows that he is Rodney King, as named in the information.[13] The accused understands the nature of the court proceedings, the roles of the various participants and the stakes and consequences involved in criminal proceedings.[14] The accused has been using the name "Captain Rod Malak Yah-Wah" since 2001, well before the events leading to the present charges. If the name in the information was changed to that name, the accused would defend the case on its merits.[15] The Court of Appeal dismissed the appeal and saw no basis to interfere with the trial judge's finding that the accused is unfit to stand trial, commenting, "Whether such an amendment can or should be made is a matter for the authorities."[16]

***R. v. Bain*, [1994] N.S.J. No. 194 (C.A.)**—That the accused's evidence was totally at odds with the instructions defence counsel received, without more, does not constitute reasonable grounds for believing the accused to be unfit to stand trial.[17]

***R. v. Bernardo* [Psychiatric Assessment Ruling], [1994] O.J. No. 4382 (Gen. Div.)**—A court may order an assessment where it has "reasonable grounds to believe" an accused may be unfit. There is no requirement that reasonable grounds be founded on expert evidence.[18]

VOLUNTARINESS OF A GUILTY PLEA

***Law Society of Upper Canada v. Tollis*, 2011 ONLSAP 44**—The standard that is applied when an appellant relies on mental disorder to invalidate a plea because of involuntariness is the same test that is used to determine the fitness of an accused to stand trial.[19]

***R. v. W. (M.A.)*, 2008 ONCA 555**—The limited cognitive capacity standard is also compatible with the test in *R. v. T. (R.)*[20] for determining the voluntariness of a guilty plea. The limited cognitive capacity standard requires an ability to understand the process and make an active or conscious choice. The standard in *T. (R.)* requires "the conscious volitional decision of the accused to plead guilty for reasons which he or she regards as appropriate." In substance, these standards are the same. Both standards require that an accused be capable of making a decision. Both standards are subjective: they reject the notion that the accused's decision must be rational or objectively in the accused's best interests.[21]

LEVEL OF FITNESS REQUIRED FOR AN EXTRADITION HEARING

***Italy v. Seifert*, 2003 BCSC 501**—Applying the test in *Whittle*, an accused must have an operating mind to be fit and, although this is an important threshold, it is not particularly high.[22] Fitness to stand trial in the context of domestic trial proceedings includes a determination of the accused's ability to instruct counsel for the purpose of a defence and this element of determination does not

13 *R. v. King*, 2007 ONCA 713 at para. 1.
14 *Ibid.* at para. 2.
15 *Ibid.* at para. 3.
16 *Ibid.* at para. 4.
17 Content reproduced with permission from *Fitness to Stand Trial*, above note 12 at Appendix A, 201.
18 *Ibid.*
19 Content reproduced with permission from *Fitness to Stand Trial*, above note 12 at Appendix A, 200.
20 *R. v. T. (R.)*, [1992] O.J. No. 1914 (C.A.).
21 *R. v. W. (M.A.)*, 2008 ONCA 555 at para. 33.
22 *Italy v. Seifert*, 2003 BCSC 501 at paras. 53, 71, and 73.

arise to the same extent in extradition committal proceedings.[23] The matters on which a person sought for extradition will need to instruct counsel are substantially less than would arise in the case of a domestic trial.[24] In extradition proceedings, the matters typically raised in defence of a committal application are technical arguments independent of instructions received from the person sought for extradition.[25]

***The Netherlands v. Mustafa*, [1999] O.J. No. 4732 (S.C.J.)**—The court applied the *Taylor* test in the context of an extradition hearing. The court was "mindful of the limited threshold that the fugitive must cross in order to be considered fit to conduct an extradition hearing" and the threshold is particularly limited since the proceedings requiring instruction are very narrow in scope and nature.[26] Notwithstanding the limited nature of the hearing, the court found that Mustafa was unfit to stand trial because he was unable to understand the nature or object of the proceedings, the possible consequences of them, or to communicate with counsel as a result of his mental disorder.[27]

* * * * *

Section 672.1(1), definitions

"accused" includes a defendant in summary conviction proceedings and an accused in respect of whom a verdict of not criminally responsible on account of mental disorder has been rendered; (*accusé*)

"assessment" means an assessment by a medical practitioner or any other person who has been designated by the Attorney General as being qualified to conduct an assessment of the mental condition of the accused under an assessment order made under section 672.11 or 672.121, and any incidental observation or examination of the accused; (*évaluation*)

"chairperson" includes any alternate that the chairperson of a Review Board may designate to act on the chairperson's behalf; (*président*)

"court" includes a summary conviction court as defined in section 785, a judge, a justice and a judge of the court of appeal as defined in section 673; (*tribunal*)

"disposition" means an order made by a court or Review Board under section 672.54, an order made by a court under section 672.58 or a finding made by a court under subsection 672.64(1); (*décision*)

"dual status offender" means an offender who is subject to a sentence of imprisonment in respect of one offence and a custodial disposition under paragraph 672.54(c) in respect of another offence; (*contrevenant à double statut*)

"high-risk accused" means an accused who is found to be a high-risk accused by a court under subsection 672.64(1); (*accusé à haut risque*)

---

23 *Ibid.* at paras. 75 and 77.

24 *Ibid.* at para. 80.

25 *Ibid.* at para. 81.

26 *The Netherlands v. Mustafa*, [1999] O.J. No. 4732 at para. 7 (S.C.J.).

27 *Ibid.* at para. 19.

"hospital" means a place in a province that is designated by the Minister of Health for the province for the custody, treatment or assessment of an accused in respect of whom an assessment order, a disposition or a placement decision is made; (*hôpital*)

CASELAW

***(C-M.), D., Re* (September 24, 2009) [2009] O.R.B.D. No. 3002 (Ont. Review Bd.)**—A detention centre is not a "hospital" within the meaning of section 672.1(1). The jurisdiction of the Review Board only permits detention orders to hospitals.

*****

"medical practitioner" means a person who is entitled to practise medicine by the laws of a province; (*médecin*)

"party" in relation to proceedings of a court or Review Board to make or review a disposition, means

(a) the accused,

(b) the person in charge of the hospital where the accused is detained or is to attend pursuant to an assessment order or a disposition,

(c) an Attorney General designated by the court or Review Board under subsection 672.5(3),

(d) any interested person designated by the court or Review Board under subsection 672.5(4), or

(e) where the disposition is to be made by a court, the prosecutor of the charge against the accused; (*parties*)

"placement decision" means a decision by a Review Board under subsection 672.68(2) as to the place of custody of a dual status offender; (*ordonnance de placement*)

"prescribed" means prescribed by regulations made by the Governor in Council under section 672.95; (*Version anglaise seulement*)

"Review Board" means the Review Board established or designated for a province pursuant to subsection 672.38(1); (*commission d'examen*)

"verdict of not criminally responsible on account of mental disorder" means a verdict that the accused committed the act or made the omission that formed the basis of the offence with which the accused is charged but is not criminally responsible on account of mental disorder. (*verdict de non-responsabilité criminelle pour cause de troubles mentaux*)

Reference

(2) For the purposes of subsections 672.5(3) and (5), paragraph 672.86(1)(b) and subsections 672.86(2) and (2.1), 672.88(2) and 672.89(2), in respect of a territory or proceedings commenced at the instance of the Government of Canada and conducted by or on behalf of that Government, a reference to the Attorney General of a province shall be read as a reference to the Attorney General of Canada.

1991, c. 43, s. 4; 2005, c. 22, s. 1; 2014, c. 6, s. 2

Defence of Mental Disorder: Section 16

16 (1) No person is criminally responsible for an act committed or an omission made while suffering from a mental disorder that rendered the person incapable of appreciating the nature and quality of the act or omission or of knowing that it was wrong.

(2) Every person is presumed not to suffer from a mental disorder so as to be exempt from criminal responsibility by virtue of subsection (1), until the contrary is proved on the balance of probabilities.

(3) The burden of proof that an accused was suffering from a mental disorder so as to be exempt from criminal responsibility is on the party that raises the issue.

R.S., 1985, c. C-46, s. 16; R.S., 1985, c. 27 (1st Supp.), s. 185(F); 1991, c. 43, s. 2.

CASELAW

MENTAL DISORDER/"DISEASE OF THE MIND"

***R. v. Luedecke*, 2008 ONCA 716**—"Mental disorder" is defined as a "disease of the mind" in section 2 of the *Criminal Code*. "Disease of the mind" is a phrase that "describes a legal and not a medical concept, the purpose of which is normative, not diagnostic." The two phrases are used interchangeably.[28]

***Canada v. Campbell*, [2000] O.J. No. 2261 (S.C.J.)**—The NCRMD (not criminally responsible on account of mental disorder) determination is a *legal* finding but what conditions are included in the legal term "disease of the mind" is a question of mixed law and fact. A holistic approach should be taken to the disease of the mind inquiry. Where a crime is committed while sleepwalking, there is a presumption that the accused suffers from a disease of the mind and the appropriate verdict is NCRMD. An acquittal will be available in only the most exceptional circumstances. In this case, the reasonable conclusion was that the accused's sleepwalking was due to an internal condition—parasomnia—that was beyond the accused's control. The trial judge accepted that the accused suffered from parasomnia and was sleepwalking at the time of the offence (a knife attack on his girlfriend). Counsel jointly agreed an NCRMD verdict was appropriate.[29]

***R. v. Parks* (1990), 78 C.R. (3d) 1 (Ont. C.A.), aff'd (1992), 15 C.R. (4th) 289 (S.C.C.)**—In order to constitute a disease of the mind under section 16(2), an illness, abnormal condition, or disorder must be shown to be the cause of the impairment of the human mind and its functioning. It must be shown that the illness, disorder, or abnormal condition caused impairment of the accused's faculties of reason, memory, and understanding at the relevant time. The defence of sleepwalking, therefore, properly falls into the category of non-insane automatism and is not a "disease of the mind." In the circumstances, the trial judge was correct in not instructing the jury as to the defence of insanity under section 16.

***R. v. Rabey* (1977), 37 C.C.C. (2d) 461, aff'd [1980] 2 S.C.R. 513**—Whether a "dissociative state" amounts to a "disease of the mind" is a question of law for the judge to determine. Medical opinions put into evidence are not determinative of the issue.

***R. v. Cooper* (1979), [1980] 1 S.C.R. 1149**—"Disease of the mind" has been given a broad definition:

> [I]n a legal sense "disease of the mind" embraces any illness, disorder or abnormal condition which impairs the human mind and its functioning, excluding however, self-induced states caused by alcohol or drugs, as well as transitory mental states such as hysteria or concussion. In order to support a defence of insanity the disease must, of course, be of such intensity as to render the accused incapable of appreciating the nature and quality of the violent act or of knowing that it is wrong.

---

28 *R. v. Luedecke*, 2008 ONCA 716 at para. 60 [*Luedecke*].

29 In footnote 4 of this case, McCombs J comments that "disease of the mind" and "mental disorder" are interchangeable terms that share the same meaning in law.

APPRECIATING AND KNOWING

***R. v. Barnier*, [1980] 1 S.C.R. 1124**—In using the two words "appreciating" and "knowing," Parliament intended that different tests be used. The verb "know" has a positive connotation and means the act of receiving information without more (requiring a base awareness), while "appreciate" requires the analysis of knowledge or experience.

NATURE AND QUALITY

***R. v. Landry*, [1991] 1 S.C.R. 99**—Appreciation of the nature and quality of the act refers to an incapacity, by reason of disease of the mind, to appreciate the physical consequences of the act.

***R. v. Kjeldsen*, [1981] 2 S.C.R. 617**—With respect to the issue of the accused's capacity to "appreciate" the nature and quality of his acts, it is correct to limit the meaning of "appreciate" to an *awareness* of the physical consequences of the act. There is no requirement for the accused to experience a normal emotional response to the physical consequences of the acts.

WRONG

***R. v. Oommen*, [1994] 2 S.C.R. 507**—The accused must have the ability to apply the knowledge that the act was wrong at the time of the otherwise criminal act. The crux of the "wrongfulness" inquiry under section 16(1) is whether the accused possessed the capacity present in the ordinary person to know that the act in question was wrong having regard to the everyday standards of the ordinary person. It must be determined whether the accused lacks the capacity to rationally decide whether the act is right or wrong and hence to make a rational choice about whether to do it. The inability to make a rational choice may result from a variety of dysfunctions and could include, for example, delusions that make the accused perceive an act that is wrong as right or justifiable and a disordered mental condition that deprives the person of the ability to rationally evaluate what they are doing.

***R. v. Ratti*, [1991] 1 S.C.R. 68**—Even if an act is motivated by a disease of the mind, such as a delusion, the accused will nonetheless be convicted if they are capable of knowing that the act in the particular circumstances would have been morally condemned by reasonable members of society.

***R. v. Chaulk*, [1990] 3 S.C.R. 1303**—"Wrong" means "morally wrong" and not simply "legally wrong."

***R. v. Schwartz*, [1977] 1 S.C.R. 673**—"Wrong" means contrary to law.

***R. v. Dobson*, 2018 ONCA 589**—"[A]n accused who, through the distorted lens of his mental illness, sees his conduct as justified, not only according to his own view, but also according to the norms of society, lacks the capacity to know that his act is wrong. That accused has an NCR defence. Similarly, an accused who, on account of mental disorder, lacks the capacity to assess the wrongfulness of his conduct against societal norms lacks the capacity to know his act is wrong and is entitled to an NCR defence."[30]

***R. v. Bharwani*, 2025 SCC 26** – While not part of the majority's decision, the minority found as follows in respect of *Dobson* at para. 222: "In sum, this Court's jurisprudence allows for an NCR verdict for an accused with a background understanding of moral wrongfulness, whose mental disorder compels them to act in a way that prevents them from applying that understanding at the moment of their criminal acts. It follows that *Dobson* impermissibly narrowed *Oommen* to the extent that it effectively reads out the capacity to choose to act, where an accused is incapable of

30 *R. v. Dobson*, 2018 ONCA 589 at para. 24.

consciously applying their knowledge that society would view their criminal act as morally wrong." The SCC's minority decision, while not part of the majority's decision, does not conflict with the majority view and will be seen as, at a minimum, persuasive.

WRONG – IN APPLICATION (CASE EXAMPLES)

***R. v. Pereira*, 2025 ONCA 545** – The trial judge rejected defence counsel's NCR argument, finding the accused responsible for homicide and entering a conviction for second degree murder. The only evidence supporting the NCR argument was from the appellant himself and the trial judge found the appellant to be an unreliable witness who lacked credibility. The trial judge expressly stated he disbelieved the accused's narrative that he acted in self-defence. The appellant failed to establish that he was incapable of knowing that what he had done was morally wrong. As set out in para. 24: "The trial judge was entitled to find that the appellant maintained the capacity to understand that the murder was morally wrong, notwithstanding his ongoing delusions."

***R v. Spencer*, [2024] B.C.J. No. 1503 (S.C.)** — In *Spencer*, the accused was found to be NCR where the uncontroverted evidence was that he, at para. 105, "was unable to rationally contemplate the wrongfulness of his actions when he ignited and reignited the fire and when he physically resisted the officers."

***R v. James*, [2024] O.J. No. 924 (S.C.J.)** — The case of *James* provides a good example of a case where there is no dispute that the accused, at para. 6:

- had a mental disorder at the time she killed her mother;
- was, at the time, experiencing symptoms of her psychotic illness;
- was, at the time, capable of appreciating the nature and quality of her conduct; and
- was, at the time, capable of knowing that her conduct was legally wrong.

The narrow issue upon which the parties disagreed was whether Ms. James was capable of knowing that her conduct was morally wrong. The expanded sequence of questions is therefore:

1) Did the accused suffer from a mental disorder at the time of the act or omission?
2) If so, was the accused, as a result of the mental disorder, either:
    i) incapable of appreciating the nature and quality of the act or omission, or
    ii) incapable of knowing that it (the act or omission) was wrong?
    iii) By "wrong"
        a) did the accused know that the act or omission was both legally and morally wrong, and
        b) did the accused have that knowledge at the time of the otherwise illegal act so as to be able to rationally apply that knowledge to their decision-making at the relevant time?

***R v. House*, [2024] O.J. No. 10 (S.C.J.)** — A similar result occurred in *House* where the uncontroverted evidence was that the accused was not able to rationally evaluate his conduct and lacked the capacity to know his act (homicide) was wrong. He was incapable of understanding that the act was wrong according to the ordinary moral standards of reasonable members of society. This was supported by the entirety of the evidence including his conduct in the moments immediately prior to chasing and killing the victim as described by witnesses, and by his mental state in the immediate aftermath of the event as demonstrated in the agreed statement of facts and video. See also: *R. v. Mahadeo*, 2024 W.C.B. 641.

See also *R. v. Khan*, 2024 ONSC 1259—The accused was found guilty but not criminally responsible. The Court concluded that it was more likely than not that the accused was suffering from a mental disorder at the time he committed the acts in question that rendered him incapable of knowing his actions were wrong.

See also *R. v. Norbu*, 2024 ONSC 3349—With respect to a first-degree murder charge, the Court found that the accused was actively psychotic at the time of the offence. The accused's psychosis — arising from his mental disorder of schizophrenia — rendered him incapable of accessing rational choice at the time he killed the victim. Due to his psychotic symptoms, the accused was unable to distinguish right from wrong.

THE SERIOUS CONSEQUENCES OF A NOT CRIMINALLY RESPONSIBLE (NCR) VERDICT

***R. v. Capano*, 2014 ONCA 599**—The consequences of an NCR finding are serious. An NCR finding places individuals in a socially protected regime that is accompanied by a significant deprivation of liberty.[31]

APPLICATION—IN GENERAL

***R. v. Ngarukiye*, 2024 QCCS 1821** — The first essential element of the NCR defence includes a question of law: whether the accused had a mental disorder (i.e., existence of mental disorder). If the evidence does not support a positive finding pertaining to a disease of the mind, then the defence cannot be opened. Once the defence is opened, it is for the jury to determine on a balance of probabilities whether the accused was suffering from a mental disorder at the time of the offence (i.e., effect of mental disorder). The prosecution's application for a jury instruction to be provided that there was no need to sequentially answer each of the two questions was denied. The prosecution's argument was at odds with the normal sequential logic with respect to the standard essential elements of any offence.

***R. v. Dobson*, 2018 ONCA 589**—In agreement with *Oommen* and its subsequent interpretations by the Ontario Court of Appeal, an accused who has the capacity to know that society regards their action as morally wrong and proceeds to commit those acts anyway has the capacity to know right from wrong and is therefore not NCR, even if they believe that they had no choice but to act or their acts were justified. If the accused—through the distorted lens of their mental illness—sees their conduct as justified in their own view *and* also according to the norms of society, then the accused lacks the capacity to know the act was wrong and has an NCR defence. Similarly, an accused who lacks the capacity to assess the wrongfulness of their conduct against societal norms because of their mental disorder is also entitled to an NCR defence.

***R. v. Campione*, 2015 ONCA 67**—Moral wrongfulness as contemplated by section 16 is a slippery concept to apply. At para. 41:

> [A] subjective but honest belief in the *justifiability* of the acts—however unreasonable that belief may be—is not sufficient, alone, to ground an NCR defence, because an individual accused's personal sense of justifiability is not sufficient. The inquiry goes further. The accused person's mental disorder must also render him or her *incapable* of knowing that the acts in question are morally wrong as measured against societal standards, and therefore incapable of making the choice necessary to act in accordance with those standards.

See *R. v. Ross*, 2009 ONCA 149 and *R. v. Woodward*, 2009 ONCA 911.

***R. v. Ross*, 2009 ONCA 149**—At para. 27, "a subjective belief by the accused that his conduct was justifiable will not spare him from criminal responsibility even if his personal views or beliefs

31 *R. v. Capano*, 2014 ONCA 599 at para. 40. The court cites *R. v. John Doe*, 2011 ONSC 92 at para. 35 and *R. v. Kankis*, 2012 ONSC 378 at paras. 1 and 20.

were driven by mental disorder, as long as he retained the capacity to know that it was wrong on a societal standard: see *Chaulk* at para. 98."

***R. v. Woodward*, 2009 ONCA 911**—The court must determine whether the accused is incapable of understanding that their acts were wrong according to the ordinary moral standards of reasonable members of the community. A result-driven approach to the NCRMD inquiry—where an expert's opinion is largely driven by the belief that the accused would be better served from a treatment perspective in the NCRMD regime than in a penitentiary—is not acceptable.

***R. v. LePage*, [1999] 2 S.C.R. 744**—The exemption arising from section 16 results in the consequence that the accused must be removed from the "normal criminal law process."[32] The nature of the NCR verdict is described in section 672.34. The accused can neither be convicted nor acquitted; it shares characteristics of both and comparisons between convicted persons and persons found NCR are "unhelpful."[33] The legislative scheme does not create any presumption of dangerousness or any presumption favouring detention pending disposition but is instead properly characterized as a "risk assessment scheme" and not a "detention review system."[34]

***R. v. Swain*, [1991] 1 S.C.R. 933**—It is recognized as a principle of fundamental justice under section 7 of the *Charter* that a person who is not criminally responsible at the time of the offence should not be convicted of it.

APPLICATION – AFTER-THE-FACT CONDUCT

***R. v. Worrie*, 2022 ONCA 471** – After-the-fact conduct may be relevant to assessing an accused's NCR defence. At para. 142:

> In the NCR context, after-the-fact conduct may be relevant to an assessment of an accused's NCR defence. Evidence, for instance, that an accused concealed the weapon or fled the scene of the offence may bear upon the accused's capacity to appreciate the wrongfulness of their conduct. At the same time, however, after-the-fact conduct is often highly ambiguous and carries the risk that the trier of fact may "mistakenly leap from such evidence to a conclusion of guilt" without taking into account alternative explanations for the accused's behaviour. Like any other evidence, after-the-fact conduct "takes on its full significance and probative value only in the context of the other evidence in the case".

APPLICATION—CASE EXAMPLES

***R. v. Huruy*, 2015 ONSC 7731**—The accused was charged with first-degree murder arising from his sudden stabbing of the victim in a café; the two had never met previously. The court was not satisfied that the murder was planned or deliberate. The court was satisfied that Huruy was guilty of second-degree murder. At the time of the offence, Huruy suffered from a mental disorder. While Huruy knew what he was doing when attacking the victim, he did not know his actions were morally wrong at the time. The question of whether someone knows their actions are morally wrong is evaluated at the time the act is committed and "[i]t is not a question at large, or of attitude generally. It is time specific."[35] The court was satisfied that Huruy did not have a rational perception of the world around him nor did he have the capacity to make rational choices arising from his

32 *R. v. LePage*, [1999] 2 S.C.R. 744 at para. 20 [*LePage* S.C.C.].

33 *Ibid.*

34 *Ibid.* at para. 46.

35 *R. v. Huruy*, 2015 ONSC 7731 at para. 19.

psychosis.[36] The court repeated that the proof for this defence is the lower standard of proof on a balance of probabilities.[37] Huruy was found not criminally responsible as a result.

***R v. Skibicki*, [2024] M.J. No. 203 (K.B.)** — It will often be the case that there is both a "mental disorder explanation" as well as an explanation that does not involve mental disorder proffered by the defence and the Crown, respectively. It will be for the trier of fact to determine the most parsimonious, compelling, explanation.

***R. v. Jackman*, 2024 ONCA 150**— The accused was convicted of criminal harassment, uttering threats, and attempted extortion in relation to his former common-law spouse. The NCR defence was rejected and the appeal from designation as a dangerous offender and the related indeterminate sentence was dismissed. With respect to the NCR defence, the rejection was reasonable because although Jackman did suffer from a mental disorder (Delusional Disorder, substance use, and Anti-Social Personality Disorder), it did not render him incapable of knowing his actions were morally wrong. In rejecting the NCR defence, the trial judge relied on Jackman's previous behaviour that was similarly abusive, dishonest, and manipulative as well as the fact that he never raised an NCR defence in prior criminal proceedings.[38] The trial judge also found that Jackman had a general disregard for societal norms, despite being aware of them. The accused's awareness of the moral wrongfulness of his actions were demonstrated by his motivations (drug use, sexual gratification, and financial gain), the content of the messages themselves, and his post-arrest conduct.[39]

ADMISSIBILITY OF EXPERT EVIDENCE

***R. v. Suarez-Noa*, 2017 ONCA 627**—The Court of Appeal allowed the appeal, set aside the acquittal, and ordered a new trial. The trial judge permitted the psychiatrist to provide opinion evidence, drawing a distinction between a "diagnosis" and a "medical explanation" for the accused's conduct. The Court of Appeal was unsure of the distinction and found that the psychiatrist provided neither; the opinion evidence did not fall within the recognized parameters of admissible psychiatric opinion evidence as to disposition.[40] The psychiatrist's opinion evidence went beyond its proper scope and the opinion was unnecessary with respect to relevance.[41] Expert opinion evidence like the kind given in this case has been rejected in several cases as an unnecessary intrusion upon the jury's responsibilities.[42]

***White Burgess Langille Inman v. Abbott and Haliburton Co.*, 2015 SCC 23**—The Supreme Court of Canada built upon existing law with respect to the expert admissibility test and held that the expert's duty to the court to provide fair, objective, and impartial opinion evidence is not only an issue of weight but is also part of the "properly qualified expert" criterion of the threshold admissibility analysis stage.

***R. v. Mohan*, [1994] 2 S.C.R. 9**—The admission of expert evidence depends on the application of four criteria at the threshold admissibility stage: (1) relevance; (2) necessity in assisting the trier

36 *Ibid.* at para. 32.

37 *Ibid.*

38 *R. v. Jackman*, 2024 ONCA 150 at para. 14.

39 *Ibid.*

40 *R. v. Suarez-Noa*, 2017 ONCA 627 at para. 84.

41 *Ibid.* at para. 85.

42 *Ibid.* at para. 86. The court cites as examples: *R. v. Lovie* (1995), 100 C.C.C. (3d) 68 at 76–78 (Ont. C.A.); *R. v. Currie* (2002), 166 C.C.C. (3d) 190 at paras. 66–67 (Ont. C.A.); *R. v. Rogers* (2005), 198 C.C.C. (3d) 449 at para. 79 (B.C.C.A.); and *R. v. Liard and Lasota*, 2013 ONSC 5457 at paras. 363–377.

of fact; (3) the absence of any exclusionary rule; and (4) a properly qualified expert. With respect to the judicial gatekeeping stage of the expert admissibility analysis, a further cost-benefit analysis is required. Logically relevant evidence may be excluded if its probative value is overborne by its prejudicial effect, if it involves an inordinate amount of time not commensurate with its value, or if it is misleading in that its effect on the trier of fact—particularly a jury—is out of proportion to its reliability.[43]

***R. v. Lavallee*, [1990] 1 S.C.R. 852**—Expert opinion is admissible, if relevant, even if based on evidence that is second-hand. Provided there exists some admissible evidence upon which to establish the foundation for the expert opinion, a trial judge cannot instruct the jury to ignore the testimony. Where the factual basis for the expert's opinion is a mixture of admissible and inadmissible evidence, the duty of the trial judge is to caution the jury that the weight to be attributed to the expert testimony is related to the amount and quality of admissible evidence upon which the opinion relies.

***R. v. Abbey*, [1982] 2 S.C.R. 24** — Medical experts are entitled to consider all possible information in forming their opinions but the party tendering that opinion evidence has the obligation of establishing the factual basis for the opinion evidence through properly admissible evidence. The facts that the opinion evidence is based on must be found to exist before the opinion evidence can be afforded any weight.

ASSESSING EXPERT EVIDENCE

***R. v. Richmond*, 2016 ONCA 134**—The jury is not obliged to accept the psychiatrist's opinion that there is a strong circumstantial case for an NCR finding, even if the opinion evidence is not contradicted by expert evidence called by the Crown. At the NCR hearing, the Crown established that the psychiatrist's opinion—which included the theory that the accused believed the victim was an imposter —rested on an incomplete foundation; the accused refused to provide a meaningful account of the offence or to permit interviews of those closest to him. The jury therefore had a rational basis to reject the expert's opinion.[44] It was also open to the jury to perceive the expert's inconsistent evidence regarding the importance of the imposter theory to the criminal responsibility opinion as "an additional discernible flaw" in that opinion.[45] In key respects, the psychiatrist's evidence was qualified and, without an account of the events from the accused, speculative.[46]

See also *R. v. Chang*, [2024] O.J. No. 2802 (C.A.) — Where there is evidence inconsistent with a finding that the accused was NCR at the relevant time, the opinion of the expert may be rejected where there is a rational basis for doing so.

See also *R. v. Langevin*, 2024 ONSC 2524 —The court saw no rational basis for rejecting the unanimous and unchallenged expert evidence, which supported an NCR finding. The expert opinion evidence in this case was supported by the evidence.

See also *R. v. Worrie* (2022), 415 C.C.C. (3d) 45 (Ont. C.A.) — There must be a rational basis for rejecting the unanimous opinion of the experts.

---

43 *R. v. Mohan*, [1994] 2 S.C.R. 9 at 20–21 [*Mohan*].

44 *R. v. Richmond*, 2016 ONCA 134 at para. 61.

45 *Ibid.* at para. 81.

46 *Ibid.* at para. 85.

***R. v. H. (W.)*, 2013 SCC 22**—The Supreme Court of Canada explains in this case and *R. v. Molodowic* that judicial experience demonstrates there is a real danger that psychiatric defences, like a mental disorder defence, are viewed by the jury with undue skepticism.[47]

***R. v. Grandbois* (2003), 174 C.C.C. (3d) 181 (Ont. C.A.)**—It is open to the jury to reject the opinions offered by psychiatrists called by the defence and to rely on other evidence about the events surrounding the shooting[48] in support of the verdict.[49] The jury is entitled to attach weight to the events surrounding the shooting.[50]

***R. v. Molodowic*, 2000 SCC 16**—The jury may reject expert opinions, even when the experts called are unanimous and uncontradicted. There must be, however, a rational foundation in the evidence for the jury to reasonably reject the expert opinions.[51] When evaluating whether a party has established the defence of mental disorder on a balance of probabilities, "[t]he nature and limits of psychiatric expertise must be kept in mind" in assessing whether the burden has been discharged.[52]

SUPPORTING EXPERT EVIDENCE NOT REQUIRED TO FIND THE ACCUSED NCRMD

***R. v. Hannah*, 2020 ONCJ 409**—The court may find an accused not criminally responsible without supporting expert evidence (or in contradiction with the available expert evidence). It is, however, highly unusual to reach a verdict of NCRMD under section 672.34 without having heard psychiatric expert evidence expressing the opinion that an NCR defence is available. It is, however, not completely unprecedented. The court further commented that merely rejecting the NCR expert opinion does not justify reaching an NCR verdict and such a result requires a conclusion that all of the requirements of section 16(1) have been met on the totality of the evidence and on a balance of probabilities.[53] The civil standard of proof involves determining what is probable, not what has been established with certainty.[54] In this case, the focus was the "wrongfulness inquiry" of the second branch of section 16(1).[55]

***R. v. Brown*, 2012 ONSC 2942**—There was a reasonable basis for finding the accused NCR, despite the report of a psychiatrist concluding that the accused was not NCR. It was clear, however, that the psychiatrist struggled with that conclusion.[56] The trial judge preferred the evidence of the complainant (which posited that he did nothing to show the accused disrespect), and concluded that the assault was unprovoked. The entirety of the facts—including a police officer observing the accused shortly after the incident and believing he was suffering from a mental health issue—had to be considered and the "circumstances giving rise to the assault cannot be viewed in a vacuum."[57]

---

47 See *R. v. H. (W.)*, 2013 SCC 22 at para. 29.

48 The accused was convicted of the second-degree murder of his wife. He admitted that he shot and killed his wife. The NCRMD defence was raised by the accused at trial. The accused did not testify. The defence called three psychiatrists who supported the NCRMD defence.

49 *R. v. Grandbois* (2003), 174 C.C.C. (3d) 181 at para. 28 (Ont. C.A.).

50 *Ibid.* at para. 35.

51 *R. v. Molodowic*, 2000 SCC 16 at paras. 8 and 12.

52 *Ibid.* at para. 15.

53 *R. v. Hannah*, 2020 ONCJ 409 at para. 16.

54 *Ibid.* at para. 17.

55 *Ibid.* at para. 16.

56 *R. v. Brown*, 2012 ONSC 2942 at para. 16.

57 *Ibid.* at para. 12.

***R. v. Quenneville*, 2010 ONCA 223** — For a trial judge's finding of NCRMD to be sustained, there still must be enough evidence — such as evidence drawn from the facts surrounding the offences and the information in the psychiatrist's report — to allow a reasonable trier to conclude on a balance of probabilities that the accused met the test in section 16(1) at the time of the offences. It is not necessary that this evidence include expert opinion evidence.[58] In this case, the accused exhibited hallucinations and delusional fantasies at the time of the offences, which were triggered by his anger and use of marijuana and Gravol. The victims also reported that the accused exhibited bizarre behaviour.[59] Taken together, this was enough for a reasonable trier to conclude on a balance of probabilities that the accused met one or both of the incapacities set out in the "wrongfulness inquiry" of the second branch of section 16(1) of the *Criminal Code*.[60]

ADEQUACY OF REASONS

As recently emphasized in *R. v. Nahmabin*[61] and *R. v. Ivins*, at para 7:[62]

> [G]iven the potential consequences of being found NCRMD – including detention in secure hospital settings that involve serious deprivations of liberty, and the possibility of lifelong supervision under Part XX.1 of the *Criminal Code* – procedural fairness must be guarded and strictly enforced in this context.

In *Nahmabin*, the trial judge improperly applied the test set out in s. 16, failed to provide a sufficient basis for her findings, and failed to provide adequate reasons. The accused's plea upon arraignment was "not criminally responsible," which is not a formal plea,[63] whereupon he was asked if the plea was "right." There was no inquiry as to whether the accused understood the plea or the ramifications of an NCR verdict which was particularly serious given the accused's repeated protestation that he did not want to be "locked-up forever" as indicated in the psychiatric report. While the facts alleged were "read-in" by the Crown, the trial judge made no actual findings of fact. There was, then, no explanation as to how any facts supported a verdict of NCR. At para. 10, the Court went on to say:

> There can be no shortcuts in a process that could result in such serious consequences to the accused. There must be a proper plea to the arraignment on the charges. Where there is agreement on the factual underpinnings of the offences, the court must nevertheless make findings with respect to the *actus reus* of the offences. The court cannot simply rely on a consent to a NCRMD finding but must first reference s.16 of the *Criminal Code* and explain why the evidence before the court justifies the NCRMD verdict.

***R. v. Ivins*, 2024 ONCA 408** — A verdict of NCR may result in indeterminate detention in a secure psychiatric facility. It is not an acquittal or a verdict somewhere in-between an acquittal and a conviction. At para. 7, therefore, a high degree of procedural fairness is required when considering the provisions pertaining to a lack of criminal responsibility.

---

58 *R. v. Quenneville*, 2010 ONCA 223 at paras. 27–28. At para. 28, the Court cites *R. v. Simpson*, [1977] O.J. No. 2264 (C.A.).

59 *Ibid.* at para. 29.

60 *Ibid.* at para. 30.

61 *R. v. Nahabin*, [2024] O.J. No. 3055 (C.A.).

62 *R. v. Ivins*, 2024 ONCA 408; See also: *R. v. Laming*, 2022 ONCA 370 at paras. 63–64; and *R. v. Capano*, 2014 ONCA 599 at paras. 45–52, 73.

63 *R. v. G. (D.M.)*, 2011 ONCA 343 at para. 43.

Ancillary Orders

Weapons Prohibitions

While the provisions of ss. 109 and 110 pertain to individuals "convicted" of an offence, the court nevertheless has discretion under s. 111 to make similar orders upon application by the Crown.

***R. v. Scheppner*, 2024 MBCA 10** — Where a person has been found NCR, they have neither been convicted nor discharged under s. 730 of the *Criminal Code* and therefore the sentencing judge does not have the jurisdiction to issue a weapons prohibition order under s. 109 of the *Criminal Code*.

DNA Data Bank

Pursuant to the provisions of ss. 487.051(3), a court may, on application of the prosecutor, if it is satisfied that it is in the best interests of the administration of justice to do so, make an order for the collection of DNA from a person found to be NCR of a primary designated offence when the verdict is rendered. See also: *R. v. Roche*, [2023] O.J. No. 2476 (C.A.) where the Court reviews the factors to be considered as set out in the section.

Sex Offender Registry

Accused obtaining a verdict of NCR are subject to the same provisions and reporting requirements as non-NCR accused convicted of a designated sexual offence. See: *R. v. M. (J.D.)* (2006), 213 C.C.C. (3d) 231 (Alta. C.A.). However, the accused may apply pursuant to the provisions of s. 490.023 of the *Code* for an exemption if certain criteria are met. See: *R. v. C. (C.)* (2008), 234 C.C.C. (3d) 389 (Alta. Prov. Ct.).

AUTOMATISM: DEFINITION AND EVIDENTIARY RULES

***R. v. Luedecke*, 2008 ONCA 716**—The distinction between non-mental disorder automatism and mental disorder automatism depends on whether the automatistic state is the product of a "mental disorder." "Mental disorder" is defined as a "disease of the mind" in section 2 of the *Criminal Code*. "Disease of the mind" is a phrase that "describes a legal and not a medical concept, the purpose of which is normative, not diagnostic." The two phrases are used interchangeably.[64] In summarizing ***R. v. Stone*, [1999] 2 S.C.R. 290**, the Court set out that the majority position in *Stone* signalled a strong preference for a finding of NCRMD in cases where an accused establishes they were in a dissociative state and acted involuntarily.[65] In this case, and others, automatistic states flowing from parasomnia were held to constitute diseases of the mind.[66]

***R. v. Stone*, [1999] 2 S.C.R. 290**—Automatism is "a state of impaired consciousness, rather than unconsciousness, in which an individual, though capable of action, has no voluntary control over that action."[67]

***R. v. Bernard*, [1988] 2 S.C.R. 833** — Intoxication or drunkenness is not in itself an excuse for crime.

***R. v. Sproule* (1975), 26 C.C.C. (2d) 92 (Ont. C.A.)** — Where the defence seeks to introduce evidence that an act was the result of automatism, such evidence should be introduced before the jury. A

64 *Luedecke*, above note 28 at para. 60.

65 *Ibid.* at para. 93.

66 *Ibid.* at para. 92. The court cited the following other cases: *Canada v. Campbell* (2000), 35 C.R. (5th) 314 (Ont. S.C.J.); *R. v. Balenko, [2000] Q.J. No. 717 (C.Q.); R. v. Romas* (2002), 6 M.V.R. (5th) 101 (B.C. Prov. Ct.); and *R. v. Churchyard* (19 November 2003), Smith J. (Ont. S.C.J.), an unreported decision.

67 *R. v. Stone*, [1999] 2 S.C.R. 290 at para. 156.

voir dire should not be resorted to where evidence is relevant and not subject to rejection on any recognized legal ground. Judges have the task of instructing the jury in their charge as to whether there was any evidence that in law would support the particular defence.

***R v. Morris*, 2024 SKCA 36**—When automatism is being raised as a defence, the question is whether there is some evidence upon which a properly instructed jury, acting judicially, could reasonably conclude that the defence has been established on a balance of probabilities. Where that threshold has been met (i.e., there is an "air or reality"), it is an error of law for the trial judge not to have left the defence with the jury.

AUTOMATISM: ADMISSIBILITY OF EXPERT EVIDENCE

***R. v. Cameron*, 2013 ONSC 1203**—The court found that the expert proposed by the Crown can be qualified as an expert in psychiatry and could give opinion evidence on the issue of automatism.[68] The court found that

> first, automatism is a comparatively rare psychiatric finding; second, there is no forensic psychiatrist in Canada who would call him/herself an expert in automatism; third, automatism is a legal term that describes in essence a type of dissociative state; and finally, there is little training or literature on the subject of automatism and much debate in the psychiatric profession concerning automatism. It is against this backdrop that Dr. Pallandi's [the psychiatrist] expertise in automatism must be assessed.[69]

The psychiatrist had never written on the subject of automatism, had never done a presentation on automatism, had never dealt with a case of automatism during his work as an investigating coroner, and had never concluded that a patient suffered from automatism while doing front-end assessments at CAMH (Centre for Addiction and Mental Health).[70] The psychiatrist testified once in a case where automatism was raised.[71] Considering all of these circumstances, the court found that the psychiatrist had some knowledge of automatism and had significant training and expertise in forensic psychiatry, the only field where automatism is studied or considered.[72]

NON-MENTAL DISORDER AUTOMATISM: THE CONSTITUTIONALITY OF SECTION 33.1 OF THE *CRIMINAL CODE*

***R. v. Brown*, 2022 SCC 18**—Section 33.1[73] of the *Criminal Code (as it then was)* violates the *Charter* and is of no force or effect pursuant to section 52(1) of the *Constitution Act, 1982.*

---

68 *R. v. Cameron*, 2013 ONSC 1203 at para. 39.

69 *Ibid.* at para. 36.

70 *Ibid.* at para. 37.

71 *Ibid.* at para. 38. The court qualifies this with the following explanation in the same paragraph: Of some importance is the fact that Dr. Pallandi initially indicated that automatism was an issue in the case in question. After cross-examination by Defence, he conceded that while automatism was discussed in that case, it was never an issue at trial. On the other hand, Dr. Pallandi stated that voluntary and conscious behaviour was at issue in that case and that these states are similar to automatism. As a result, I find that Dr. Pallandi has never testified in court on the issue of automatism *per se* although he has testified on similar issues.

72 *Ibid.* at para. 39.

73 Section 33.1 sets out that non-mental disorder automatism is not a defence if the automatism is: (1) self-induced by voluntary intoxication and (2) the offence charged is a violence-based offence. This applies to general and specific intent offences and was enacted by Parliament in 1995 in response to the public outcry with respect to *R. v. Daviault*, [1994] 3 S.C.R. 63. The *Daviault* case created a pathway to exoneration for general intent offences through extreme intoxication.

Note: This appeal is a companion case to ***R. v. Sullivan*, 2022 SCC 19**, a Crown appeal to the Supreme Court of Canada from two different cases (*R. v. Chan*, 2022 SCC 19 and *Sullivan*) heard together where the Court of Appeal for Ontario found the same.

***R. v. Sullivan*, 2020 ONCA 333, aff'd 2022 SCC 19**—The conclusion reached in ***R. v. Brown*, 2022 SCC 18**, is applicable to these cases. Section 33.1 of the *Criminal Code* infringes sections 7 and 11(d) of the *Charter*, cannot be saved under section 1, and is of no force and effect. Non-mental disorder automatism can therefore potentially be an available defence even if self-induced by voluntary intoxication and the offence is violent. This case adjudicated upon two separate, unrelated incidents involving two accused (Chan and Sullivan), where both men attacked and stabbed loved ones while in drug-induced psychoses. Neither had any discernible motive. On appeal to the Court of Appeal for Ontario, both argued that section 33.1 of the *Criminal Code* unconstitutionally deprived them of accessing the non-mental disorder automatism defence. For Sullivan, acquittals were entered. For Chan, a new trial was ordered. Leave to appeal to the Supreme Court of Canada was granted on 3 June 2020 in ***Her Majesty the Queen, et al. v. David Sullivan, et al.*, [2020] S.C.C.A. No. 232**. The Supreme Court of Canada heard the case in October 2021 and affirmed the finding of the Court of Appeal for Ontario.

NON-MENTAL DISORDER AUTOMATISM: NEW LEGISLATION ENACTED ON 23 JUNE 2022 IN RESPONSE TO THE DECISIONS OF THE SUPREME COURT OF CANADA

As a result of the decisions in ***R. v. Brown*, 2022 SCC 18** and ***R. v. Sullivan*, 2022 SCC 19**, Parliament enacted new legislation that changed section 33.1 of the *Criminal Code* to the text set out below to further narrow the availability of the defence of non-mental disorder automatism arising from self-induced extreme intoxication.

Offences of violence by negligence
33.1 (1) A person who, by reason of self-induced extreme intoxication, lacks the general intent or voluntariness ordinarily required to commit an offence referred to in subsection (3), nonetheless commits the offence if

(a) all the other elements of the offence are present; and
(b) before they were in a state of extreme intoxication, they departed markedly from the standard of care expected of a reasonable person in the circumstances with respect to the consumption of intoxicating substances.

Marked departure—foreseeability of risk and other circumstances
(2) For the purposes of determining whether the person departed markedly from the standard of care, the court must consider the objective foreseeability of the risk that the consumption of the intoxicating substances could cause extreme intoxication and lead the person to harm another person. The court must, in making the determination, also consider all relevant circumstances, including anything that the person did to avoid the risk.

Offences
(3) This section applies in respect of an offence under this Act or any other Act of Parliament that includes as an element an assault or any other interference or threat of interference by a person with the bodily integrity of another person.

Definition of *extreme intoxication*
(4) In this section, *extreme intoxication* means intoxication that renders a person unaware of, or incapable of consciously controlling, their behaviour.

INEFFECTIVE ASSISTANCE OF COUNSEL

***R. v. Costa*, 2017 ONSC 2044**—A taxi driver activated his vehicle's emergency help button when the accused smoked crack in the vehicle. Police found less than four grams of crack cocaine on the accused. At the time, the accused was subject to a recognizance of bail with the term that he was not to consume or possess non-medically prescribed drugs. The accused repeatedly made statements that he had official immunity from prosecution for possessing and smoking crack, showing that he had mental health problems. The accused was found fit. An assessment report concluded that the accused was not criminally responsible by virtue of his suffering from schizophrenia and cocaine dependence disorder at the time of the offences. The accused did not know the legal and moral wrongfulness of his actions. The accused was found NCR and detained. His appeal, alleging ineffective assistance of counsel, was dismissed. The accused failed to prove that prejudice or a miscarriage of justice resulted by the conduct of trial counsel. The court held that the NCR order would have been made even if trial counsel did what the accused alleged should have been done.

***R. v. Bailey*, 2022 ONCA 507** — When the NCR accused is not aware of the implications of an NCR outcome and is not aware of his related appeal rights from an NCR finding due to ineffective assistance of counsel, the interests of justice require the granting of an extension of time to bring an appeal even in the face of an extraordinary delay, if the delay is adequately explained. In this case, the extraordinary delay was a duration of seven years between the time the accused was found NCR (a defence application that was consented to by the Crown) and the time when the accused learned of his option to appeal the NCR verdict.

TIMING OF THE NCRMD DEFENCE

***R. v. Richmond*, 2016 ONCA 134**—The accused was convicted by jury of the second-degree murder of his wife and then raised the NCRMD defence. The jury rejected the NCMRD defence at the NCR hearing. The jury's verdict was not unreasonable. There was no procedural unfairness to the accused arising from the psychiatrist's failure to interview the accused after his conviction and before the NCR hearing. The timing of the defence disclosure that it intended to raise the criminal responsibility issue was within the control of the defence.[74] There was no claim of hearing unfairness or prejudice to the accused in relation to the NCR hearing.[75]

ADVERSE INFERENCE

***R. v. Sweeney (No. 2)*, [1977] O.J. No. 2353 (C.A.); *R. v. Worth*, [1995] O.J. No. 1063 (C.A.)**—While an accused asserting a defence of NCR is not obligated to submit to an examination by a psychiatrist retained by the Crown, an adverse inference may be drawn from a failure to do so.

APPLICATION—MISTRIAL

***R. v. Chen*, 2019 ONSC 3088**—A mistrial cannot be granted on the basis of speculation. Where the defence seeks a mistrial to allow for time to make inquiries into whether a forensic psychiatrist might be found to support their "not criminally responsible" defence, then no mistrial is warranted.

---

74 *R. v. Richmond*, 2016 ONCA 134 at para. 91.
75 *Ibid.* at para. 90.

INFANTICIDE UNDER SECTION 233 OF THE *CRIMINAL CODE*—"DISTURBED MIND"

***R. v. Borowiec*, 2016 SCC 11**—The phrase "her mind is then disturbed" in section 233 of the *Criminal Code* legally means that the disturbance must be "by reason" of a woman not having fully recovered from the effects of giving birth or the effect of lactation. Having a "disturbed" mind does not require evidence that the accused has a mental disorder. Parliamentary intent with respect to the concept of a "disturbed" mind is to have its ordinary meaning in order to provide a broad and flexible legal standard that would serve the ends of justice. In this case, the trial judge applied the correct standard to the law of infanticide in concluding that the accused's mind was "disturbed" as a result of her not having fully recovered from the effects of giving birth. The Crown's argument that the mother only had a "disturbed" mind if her psychological health was "substantially compromised" because she recently gave birth is too high a standard and contrary to parliamentary intention. There was an evidentiary basis for the trial judge to conclude that the Crown failed to prove that the accused's mind was not disturbed at the time of the offences.

***R. v. B. (L.)*, 2011 ONCA 153, leave to appeal to the S.C.C. ref'd 2011 CarswellOnt 3519 (S.C.C.)**—The accused was acquitted of first-degree murder and convicted of infanticide, with the trial judge concluding that disturbance was sufficient to afford a defence of infanticide. The Crown's appeal was dismissed. The trial judge returned proper verdicts. The *mens rea* for infanticide cannot be equated with the *mens rea* for murder. In cases where infanticide is raised as a defence, the jury must decide the nature of culpable homicide and should be told to consider infanticide first. If the Crown fails to negate at least one element of infanticide beyond a reasonable doubt, the jury should be instructed to return a verdict of not guilty of murder but guilty of infanticide. In this case, the trial judge found that both homicides met the criteria for infanticide, negating the Crown's argument that at least one of the elements of infanticide was not proven beyond a reasonable doubt. Infanticide is a partial defence to a murder charge.

* * * * *

Assessment Orders

Assessment order

672.11 A court having jurisdiction over an accused in respect of an offence may order an assessment of the mental condition of the accused, if it has reasonable grounds to believe that such evidence is necessary to determine

(a) whether the accused is unfit to stand trial;

(b) whether the accused was, at the time of the commission of the alleged offence, suffering from a mental disorder so as to be exempt from criminal responsibility by virtue of subsection 16(1);

(c) whether the balance of the mind of the accused was disturbed at the time of commission of the alleged offence, where the accused is a female person charged with an offence arising out of the death of her newly-born child;

(d) the appropriate disposition to be made, where a verdict of not criminally responsible on account of mental disorder or unfit to stand trial has been rendered in respect of the accused;

(d.1) whether a finding that the accused is a high-risk accused should be revoked under subsection 672.84(3); or

(e) whether an order should be made under section 672.851 for a stay of proceedings, where a verdict of unfit to stand trial has been rendered against the accused.

1991, c. 43, s. 4; 1995, c. 22, s. 10; 2005, c. 22, s. 2; 2014, c. 6, s. 3

CASELAW

APPLICATION — REASONABLE GROUNDS STANDARD

***John Doe, R.*, 2011 ONSC 92**—An accused's history with respect to fitness assessments and previous encounters with police may suggest the "possibility" that he was not criminally responsible but section 672.12(3)(b) requires more for a court to make an assessment order under section 672.11 on the section 16 (NCRMD—not criminally responsible on account of mental disorder) issue. The standard is not one of "possibility"; the standard is reasonable grounds to believe that a mental disorder rendered the accused incapable of appreciating the nature and quality of their conduct or knowing that it was wrong.

***R. v. B. (B.)*, [2009] O.J. No. 863 (S.C.J.)**—Where the expert opinion is that the accused is choosing not to answer questions regarding the trial process and is generally uncooperative with counsel, and while there is no indication of a mental disorder, the threshold for ordering a fitness assessment has not been met.[76]

***R. v. Bernardo* [Psychiatric Assessment Ruling], [1994] O.J. No. 4382 (Gen. Div.)**—A court may order an assessment where it has "reasonable grounds to believe" an accused may be unfit. There is no requirement that reasonable grounds be founded on expert evidence.[77]

APPLICATION — EVIDENTIARY APPROACH

***R. v. Isaac*, 2009 ONCJ 662**—At para. 3:

> Section **672.11** of the ***Criminal Code*** sets out various issues in respect of which Assessment Orders may be made. They are: a) fitness to stand trial; b) criminal responsibility; c) infanticide; d) least onerous, least restrictive disposition; and e) stay of proceedings for permanently unfit accused. The subject or focus of the assessment is limited to the "mental condition of the accused". An Assessment Order may only be made where the court has reasonable grounds to believe that an assessment of the accused's *mental condition* is necessary to determine whether the accused is (in this case) unfit to stand trial. *While the Code is silent as to what might take the court to the point of "reasonable grounds to believe", it is clear that no particular evidence is necessary.* Nevertheless, the basis for the belief must be clear and plainly appear on the record of proceedings. The court may make an Assessment Order at any stage of the proceedings on its own motion or that of either party" [emphasis added].

***R. v. Muschke*, [1997] B.C.J. No. 2825 (S.C.)**—This case employed a stricter approach than ***R. v. Isaac*, 2009 ONCJ 662**, insisting on sworn evidence to establish reasonable grounds to make an assessment order. At para. 40:

> In the ordinary course, evidence on an application before a court is provided by way of affidavit and, occasionally, by oral testimony. Notwithstanding that the practice on applications in criminal matters may be more flexible than that in civil matters, I see no reason why reasonable grounds for doubt, as required by s. 672.12, should be derived from the statements of counsel alone without affidavit or *viva voce* evidence and satisfactory medical opinion.[78]

---

76 Content reproduced with permission from *Fitness to Stand Trial*, above note 12 at Appendix A, 201.

77 *Ibid.*

78 Note that assessment orders are routinely made upon the submissions of counsel, contents of police reports, or observations of the accused in the courtroom.

***R. v. Lojovic*, 2025 ONCA 319** – If an application to order an NCR assessment arises after a trial judge delivers their reasons for conviction after hearing all of the evidence at trial, then the trial judge can appropriately rely upon the trial evidence to reject the application. In this case, the trial judge did not consider a further assessment under s. 672.11 necessary to determine criminal responsibility as the trial judge had the benefit of hearing the trial evidence. It was evident that the NCR application was based upon the trial evidence as counsel did not call any additional evidence nor request such an opportunity. On appeal, counsel did not bring a fresh evidence motion nor did counsel demonstrate that the trial judge erred in finding that the trial evidence did not provide reasonable grounds to believe that an NCR assessment would be necessary.

APPLICATION—NON-COMPLIANCE WITH ASSESSMENT ORDER

***R. v. Brown*, 2015 ONSC 3211**—The accused was remanded under section 672.11 for assessment of his mental condition to permit the court to consider the issue of the accused's criminal responsibility. The accused refused to be assessed unless the interviews were audio recorded and, as a result, the attending psychiatrist could not complete an assessment.[79] The court accepted the psychiatrists' opinion that the most reliable assessment could only be obtained through a thorough evaluation. The court found that a period of hospitalization was required for that purpose.[80] The court concluded that its original order had not been complied with and issued another order under section 672.11.[81]

Related Provisions: Section 672.11 provides for an assessment order being made of a person charged with an offence arising out of the death of their newly born child, which could include a broad set of offences. One included offence is infanticide, under section 233 of the *Criminal Code*. Both sections contemplate the situation where a female person's mind is disturbed at the time of the commission of the offence. The caselaw under section 233 of the *Criminal Code* addressing the meaning of a "disturbed mind" in this context is therefore helpful in defining what is meant when an assessment order is made to determine whether the "balance of the mind of the accused was disturbed" under section 672.11.

*****

Where court may order assessment

672.12 (1) The court may make an assessment order at any stage of proceedings against the accused of its own motion, on application of the accused or, subject to subsections (2) and (3), on application of the prosecutor.

Limitation on prosecutor's application for assessment of fitness

(2) Where the prosecutor applies for an assessment in order to determine whether the accused is unfit to stand trial for an offence that is prosecuted by way of summary conviction, the court may only order the assessment if

(a) the accused raised the issue of fitness; or

(b) the prosecutor satisfies the court that there are reasonable grounds to doubt that the accused is fit to stand trial.

---

79 *R. v. Brown*, 2015 ONSC 3211 at para. 15.

80 *Ibid.* at para. 35.

81 *Ibid.* at para. 36.

Limitation on prosecutor's application for assessment

(3) Where the prosecutor applies for an assessment in order to determine whether the accused was suffering from a mental disorder at the time of the offence so as to be exempt from criminal responsibility, the court may only order the assessment if

(a) the accused puts his or her mental capacity for criminal intent into issue; or

(b) the prosecutor satisfies the court that there are reasonable grounds to doubt that the accused is criminally responsible for the alleged offence, on account of mental disorder.

1991, c. 43, s. 4

CASELAW

***R. v. Vassell*, 2013 ONCJ 333**—Crown application, prior to trial, to assess the accused with respect to criminal responsibility dismissed as premature. Referred to ***R. v. Swain*, [1991] 1 S.C.R. 933**, in finding that either of the two statutory conditions must first be satisfied.

* * * * *

Review Board may order assessment

672.121 The Review Board that has jurisdiction over an accused found not criminally responsible on account of mental disorder or unfit to stand trial may order an assessment of the mental condition of the accused of its own motion or on application of the prosecutor or the accused, if it has reasonable grounds to believe that such evidence is necessary to

(a) make a recommendation to the court under subsection 672.851(1);

(b) make a disposition under section 672.54 in one of the following circumstances:

  (i) no assessment report on the mental condition of the accused is available,

  (ii) no assessment of the mental condition of the accused has been conducted in the last twelve months, or

  (iii) the accused has been transferred from another province under section 672.86; or

(c) determine whether to refer to the court for review under subsection 672.84(1) a finding that an accused is a high-risk accused.

2005, c. 22, s. 3; 2014, c. 6, s. 4

CASELAW

PAYMENT OF INDEPENDENT PSYCHIATRIC ASSESSMENTS

***Ontario (Attorney General) v. Ontario (Review Board)*, 2010 ONCA 35**—The Ontario Review Board lacks the jurisdiction under Part XX.1 of the *Criminal Code* to order the Attorney General, or any other party, to pay for an independent psychiatric assessment. The case did not involve any *Charter* values.

TREATMENT IMPASSES

***Gonzalez, Re*, 2017 ONCA 102**[82]—At para. 40, "If the only way forward for the appellant is for him to consent to treatment or be declared incapable, and the appellant's mental illness precludes his consent to treatment, but the team has not declared him incapable, then a treatment impasse

82 Application for leave submitted to the SCC on 22 January 2018 in *Gonzalez v. Person in Charge of Waypoint Centre for Mental Health* Care, 2017 CarswellOnt 21193 (S.C.C.), leave to appeal to S.C.C. refused [2017] S.C.C.A. No. 135.

plainly exists." A long period of incarceration without treatment or progress can constitute a treatment impasse.[83] When evidence suggests that a treatment impasse might have been reached, the Board is obliged to consider that possibility. It is an error in law for the Board to adopt an approach that refuses to recognize a treatment impasse and to be complacent by leaving any future progress up to the accused.[84]

***R. v. Conway*, 2008 ONCA 326**—It is an error of law and unreasonable for the Board to not impose conditions to address the accused's lack of progress/treatment impasse over his twenty-four-year detention. See para. 67.

***Mazzei v. British Columbia (Director of Adult Forensic Psychiatric Services)*, 2006 SCC 7**—The Board is obliged to consider the possibility of a treatment impasse as part of its inquisitorial function. This case sets out the principles related to the determination of a treatment impasse. Review Boards have the power to bind hospital authorities and impose conditions. As part of its supervisory powers, the Board is entitled to order a re-evaluation of current or past treatment approaches and an exploration of alternatives. The Board has authority to order an independent assessment under section 672.121 (see para. 39 and ***Runnalis, Re*, 2012 ONCA 295 at para. 14**). See also ***R. v. LePage*, [2006] O.J. No. 4486 (C.A.) at paras. 23–26**, and ***R. v. Conway*, [2008] O.J. No. 1588 (C.A.) at paras. 29–34, Armstrong J.A., and at paras. 67 and 83–85, Lang J.A.**

***R. v. LePage*, [2006] O.J. No. 4486 (C.A.)**—LePage languished for twenty-eight years, refusing treatment. The danger posed to the public remained unchanged and LePage was receiving no treatment because of his unwillingness to engage. In this case, it was unclear what might break the impasse or if the impasse could be broken but after twenty-eight years, it was incumbent on the Board to consider making further inquiry. The Board's burden to search out and consider evidence extends to evidence favouring the restriction of the NCR accused as well as evidence in his favour, regardless of whether the NCR accused is present.[85]

* * * * *

Contents of assessment order

672.13 (1) An assessment order must specify

(a) the service that or the person who is to make the assessment, or the hospital where it is to be made;

(b) whether the accused is to be detained in custody while the order is in force; and

(c) the period that the order is to be in force, including the time required for the assessment and for the accused to travel to and from the place where the assessment is to be made.

Form

(2) An assessment order may be in Form 48 or 48.1.

1991, c. 43, s. 4; 2005, c. 22, s. 4

General rule for period

672.14 (1) An assessment order shall not be in force for more than thirty days.

83 *Gonzalez, Re*, 2017 ONCA 102 at para. 28.

84 *Ibid.* at para. 40.

85 *R. v. LePage*, [2006] O.J. No. 4486 at para. 22 (C.A.) [*LePage* (C.A.)].

CASELAW

PARLIAMENTARY INTENT: ASSESSMENTS TO BE COMPLETED WITH DISPATCH

***Phaneuf v. Ontario*, 2010 ONCA 901**—From para. 16:

> Assessment orders are time limited. Generally speaking, they are in force for no more than 30 days. In addition, a person must be returned to the court forthwith after the assessment is completed: *Criminal Code* ss. 672.14, 672.15 and 672.17. Taken together, the sections clearly indicate Parliament's intention that assessments ordered under s. 672.11 should be completed with dispatch.

* * * * *

Exception in fitness cases
(2) No assessment order to determine whether the accused is unfit to stand trial shall be in force for more than five days, excluding holidays and the time required for the accused to travel to and from the place where the assessment is to be made, unless the accused and the prosecutor agree to a longer period not exceeding thirty days.

Exception for compelling circumstances
(3) Despite subsections (1) and (2), a court or Review Board may make an assessment order that remains in force for sixty days if the court or Review Board is satisfied that compelling circumstances exist that warrant it.
1991, c. 43, s. 4; 2005, c. 22, s. 5

Extension
672.15 (1) Subject to subsection (2), a court or Review Board may extend an assessment order, of its own motion or on the application of the accused or the prosecutor made during or at the end of the period during which the order is in force, for any further period that is required, in its opinion, to complete the assessment of the accused.

Maximum duration of extensions
(2) No extension of an assessment order shall exceed thirty days, and the period of the initial order together with all extensions shall not exceed sixty days.
1991, c. 43, s. 4; 2005, c. 22, s. 6

CASE LAW

***R. v. Nichols*, 2024 ONSC 1602** — Sections 672.14 and 672.15 provide a maximum of 60 days for assessments, including any extensions. In this case, the circumstances favoured granting a further fitness assessment order, though a fitness assessment had been underway for 60 days pursuant to a court order. The circumstances favouring a further fitness assessment order were the case was serious (murder), the accused's custody status was not impacted, the psychiatric issues are complex, and the defence is seeking the further order unopposed. At para. 29, the Court concluded that it had jurisdiction to grant a further assessment order; the 60-day period had elapsed, but the courts have jurisdiction to order an additional assessment under sections 672.11, 672.14 and 672.15. A new 30-day fitness assessment was granted. The court finds that the provisions of the *Criminal Code* must be given a large and liberal interpretation to ensure the court has the necessary evidence to assess the accused's fitness to stand trial. In this case, the complexity of the psychiatric issues and the specialized work remaining to permit completion of the assessment resulted in the elapse of 60 days. Resourcing issues did not cause delays.

***R. v. Reimer*, 2022 MBKB 183** — The court found that it had jurisdiction to grant a second assessment order under s. 672. A first assessment order was granted and extended, but the order expired before being implemented due to a lack of available beds at the forensic assessment centre. To determine the NCR issue, the Court reasoned that a large and liberal interpretation should be applied to the assessment order provisions as a strict reading would cause injustice. The availability of hospital beds or medical personnel falls under the purview of the hospital, as the court has no ability to control the hospitals or medical personnel who conduct assessments. Nothing in s. 672.11 restricts the number of orders that can be granted.

Presumption against custody

672.16 (1) Subject to subsection (3), an accused shall not be detained in custody under an assessment order of a court unless

(a) the court is satisfied that on the evidence custody is necessary to assess the accused, or that on the evidence of a medical practitioner custody is desirable to assess the accused and the accused consents to custody;

(b) custody of the accused is required in respect of any other matter or by virtue of any other provision of this Act; or

(c) the prosecutor, having been given a reasonable opportunity to do so, shows that detention of the accused in custody is justified on either of the grounds set out in subsection 515(10).

Presumption against custody—Review Board

(1.1) If the Review Board makes an order for an assessment of an accused under section 672.121, the accused shall not be detained in custody under the order unless

(a) the accused is currently subject to a disposition made under paragraph 672.54(c);

(b) the Review Board is satisfied on the evidence that custody is necessary to assess the accused, or that on the evidence of a medical practitioner custody is desirable to assess the accused and the accused consents to custody; or

(c) custody of the accused is required in respect of any other matter or by virtue of any other provision of this Act.

Residency as a condition of disposition

(1.2) Subject to paragraphs (1.1) (b) and (c), if the accused is subject to a disposition made under paragraph 672.54(b) that requires the accused to reside at a specified place, an assessment ordered under section 672.121 shall require the accused to reside at the same place.

Report of medical practitioner

(2) For the purposes of paragraphs (1)(a) and (1.1)(b), if the prosecutor and the accused agree, the evidence of a medical practitioner may be received in the form of a report in writing.

Presumption of custody in certain circumstances

(3) An assessment order made in respect of an accused who is detained under subsection 515(6) or 522(2) shall order that the accused be detained in custody under the same circumstances referred to in that subsection, unless the accused shows that custody is not justified under the terms of that subsection.

1991, c. 43, s. 4; 2005, c. 22, s. 7

Assessment order takes precedence over bail hearing

672.17 During the period that an assessment order made by a court in respect of an accused charged with an offence is in force, no order for the interim release or detention of the accused may be made by virtue of Part XVI or section 679 in respect of that offence or an included offence.

1991, c. 43, s. 4; 2005, c. 22, s. 8

Application to vary assessment order

672.18 Where at any time while an assessment order made by a court is in force the prosecutor or an accused shows cause, the court may vary the terms of the order respecting the interim release or detention of the accused in such manner as it considers appropriate in the circumstances.

1991, c. 43, s. 4; 2005, c. 22, s. 9(F)

No treatment order on assessment

672.19 No assessment order may direct that psychiatric or any other treatment of the accused be carried out or direct the accused to submit to such treatment.

1991, c. 43, s. 4

When assessment completed

672.191 An accused in respect of whom an assessment order is made shall appear before the court or Review Board that made the order as soon as practicable after the assessment is completed and not later than the last day of the period that the order is to be in force.

1997, c. 18, s. 81; 2005, c. 22, s. 10

ASSESSMENT REPORTS

Assessment report

672.2 (1) An assessment order may require the person who makes the assessment to submit in writing an assessment report on the mental condition of the accused.

Assessment report to be filed

(2) An assessment report shall be filed with the court or Review Board that ordered it, within the period fixed by the court or Review Board, as the case may be.

Court to send assessment report to Review Board

(3) The court shall send to the Review Board without delay a copy of any report filed with it pursuant to subsection (2), to assist in determining the appropriate disposition to be made in respect of the accused.

Copies of reports to accused and prosecutor

(4) Subject to subsection 672.51(3), copies of any report filed with a court or Review Board under subsection (2) shall be provided without delay to the prosecutor, the accused and any counsel representing the accused.

1991, c. 43, s. 4; 2005, c. 22, s. 11

PROTECTED STATEMENTS

Definition of protected statement

672.21 (1) In this section, protected statement means a statement made by the accused during the course and for the purposes of an assessment or treatment directed by a disposition, to the person specified in the assessment order or the disposition, or to anyone acting under that person's direction.

Protected statements not admissible against accused

(2) No protected statement or reference to a protected statement made by an accused is admissible in evidence, without the consent of the accused, in any proceeding before a court, tribunal, body or person with jurisdiction to compel the production of evidence.

Exceptions

(3) Notwithstanding subsection (2), evidence of a protected statement is admissible for the purpose of

(a) determining whether the accused is unfit to stand trial;

(b) making a disposition or placement decision respecting the accused;

(c) determining, under section 672.84, whether to refer to the court for review a finding that an accused is a high-risk accused or whether to revoke such a finding;

(d) determining whether the balance of the mind of the accused was disturbed at the time of commission of the alleged offence, where the accused is a female person charged with an offence arising out of the death of her newly-born child;

(e) determining whether the accused was, at the time of the commission of an alleged offence, suffering from automatism or a mental disorder so as to be exempt from criminal responsibility by virtue of subsection 16(1), if the accused puts his or her mental capacity for criminal intent into issue, or if the prosecutor raises the issue after verdict;

(f) challenging the credibility of an accused in any proceeding where the testimony of the accused is inconsistent in a material particular with a protected statement that the accused made previously; or

(g) establishing the perjury of an accused who is charged with perjury in respect of a statement made in any proceeding.

1991, c. 43, s. 4; 2005, c. 22, s. 12; 2014, c. 6, s. 5

Fitness to Stand Trial

Presumption of fitness

672.22 An accused is presumed fit to stand trial unless the court is satisfied on the balance of probabilities that the accused is unfit to stand trial.

1991, c. 43, s. 4

Court may direct issue to be tried

672.23 (1) Where the court has reasonable grounds, at any stage of the proceedings before a verdict is rendered, to believe that the accused is unfit to stand trial, the court may direct, of its own motion or on application of the accused or the prosecutor, that the issue of fitness of the accused be tried.

Burden of proof

(2) An accused or a prosecutor who makes an application under subsection (1) has the burden of proof that the accused is unfit to stand trial.

1991, c. 43, s. 4

CASELAW

THE ISSUE OF FITNESS ARISING AFTER THE VERDICT

***R. v. Morrison*, 2016 SKQB 259**—The applicant faced a dangerous offender application after being convicted of break and enter and sexual assault causing bodily harm. The defence ordered a fitness assessment, which concluded that the accused was not fit. The court granted the "reading-in remedy" sought by defence counsel, allowing for the fitness hearing to occur post-verdict as the language of the impugned provisions violated the accused's section 7 *Charter* rights and were not justified under section 1 of the *Charter*. The court found it was necessary that the accused be able to instruct counsel during the dangerous offender sentencing hearing.

***R. v. Jaser*, 2015 ONSC 4729**—This case involved two co-accused, Jaser and Esseghaier. After a jury trial, convictions were entered for both accused for offences of conspiracy to derail a passenger train for the benefit of a terrorist group and conspiracy to commit murder for the benefit of a terrorist group. During the sentencing hearing, the issue arose as to whether the court should inquire into Esseghaier's fitness by ordering a psychiatric assessment. Esseghaier consented to a psychiatric assessment under section 21 of the Ontario *Mental Health Act* as there was no provision in the *Criminal Code* providing for a psychiatric assessment pending sentence. The court found that section 7 of the *Charter* requires that a trial judge possess the power to inquire into the "limited cognitive capacity" or "operating mind" of the accused at a sentencing hearing but that extending sections 2 and 672.23(1) by a "reading in" remedy in *R. v. B. (G.)* was not appropriate as it would give rise to significant criminal law policy questions and would require amendments to sections 672.38 and 672.47 of the *Criminal Code* to expand the jurisdiction of the Review Board. The court made a further section 21 assessment order to address the issue of Esseghaier's fitness at a sentencing hearing.

***R. v. B. (G.)*, [2003] O.J. No. 784 (S.C.J.)**[86] — The Crown brought a dangerous offender application after the accused was convicted of several charges of assault, sexual assault, unlawful confinement, and criminal harassment against his girlfriend. Following the verdict but before sentencing, the accused became unfit to communicate with counsel, who brought an application arguing that sections 2 and 672.23(1) of the *Criminal Code* violated section 7 of the *Charter* since it addressed only the issue to stand trial and did not provide for unfitness during sentencing. The application was granted, and the court found that the "legislative gap" violated the accused's section 7 *Charter* right. The accused's ability to participate in the dangerous offender application was essential. The infringement was not justified under section 1 of the *Charter*. At para. 48, the remedy ordered was to "read-in" the words "at any stage of the proceedings before a verdict is rendered or sentence imposed."

* * * * *

Counsel

672.24 (1) Where the court has reasonable grounds to believe that an accused is unfit to stand trial and the accused is not represented by counsel, the court shall order that the accused be represented by counsel.

CASELAW

***R. v. Savard*, [1996] Y.J. No. 4 (C.A.), refusing leave to appeal *Alain Savard v. Attorney General of Canada*, [1996] S.C.C.A. No. 297**—The court does not have the power under this section of the *Criminal Code* to order the Attorney General to pay a lawyer's account who is representing the accused by order under section 672.24 of the *Criminal Code*.

***R. v. Waranuk* (2010), Y.J. No. 81 (C.A.)**—The entitlement to counsel arises at the time of an application for an assessment order to determine the issue of fitness to stand trial.

* * * * *

86 This case is also referred to as *R. v. Balliram* in the caselaw.

Counsel fees and disbursements

(2) Where counsel is assigned pursuant to subsection (1) and legal aid is not granted to the accused pursuant to a provincial legal aid program, the fees and disbursements of counsel shall be paid by the Attorney General to the extent that the accused is unable to pay them.

Taxation of fees and disbursements

(3) Where counsel and the Attorney General cannot agree on the fees or disbursements of counsel, the Attorney General or the counsel may apply to the registrar of the court and the registrar may tax the disputed fees and disbursements.

1991, c. 43, s. 4; 1997, c. 18, s. 82

Postponing trial of issue

672.25 (1) The court shall postpone directing the trial of the issue of fitness of an accused in proceedings for an offence for which the accused may be prosecuted by indictment or that is punishable on summary conviction, until the prosecutor has elected to proceed by way of indictment or summary conviction.

Idem

(2) The court may postpone directing the trial of the issue of fitness of an accused

(a) where the issue arises before the close of the case for the prosecution at a preliminary inquiry, until a time that is not later than the time the accused is called on to answer to the charge; or

(b) where the issue arises before the close of the case for the prosecution at trial, until a time not later than the opening of the case for the defence or, on motion of the accused, any later time that the court may direct.

1991, c. 43, s. 4

CASELAW

***R. v. Le*, [2004] O.J. No. 3374 (C.J.)**—Where an accused disputes the Crown's ability to show a *prima facie* case prior to a trial of fitness to stand trial, this may be done in a relatively informal manner by calling the officer in charge to indicate what witnesses remain ready to testify and the sorts of evidence they will be producing.[87]

*****

Trial of issue by judge and jury

672.26 Where an accused is tried or is to be tried before a court composed of a judge and jury,

(a) if the judge directs that the issue of fitness of the accused be tried before the accused is given in charge to a jury for trial on the indictment, a jury composed of the number of jurors required in respect of the indictment in the province where the trial is to be held shall be sworn to try that issue and, with the consent of the accused, the issues to be tried on the indictment; and

(b) if the judge directs that the issue of fitness of the accused be tried after the accused has been given in charge to a jury for trial on the indictment, the jury shall be sworn to try that issue in addition to the issues in respect of which it is already sworn.

1991, c. 43, s. 4

87 Content reproduced with permission from *Fitness to Stand Trial*, above note 12 at Appendix A, 208.

Trial of issue by court

672.27 The court shall try the issue of fitness of an accused and render a verdict where the issue arises

(a) in respect of an accused who is tried or is to be tried before a court other than a court composed of a judge and jury; or

(b) before a court at a preliminary inquiry or at any other stage of the proceedings.

1991, c. 43, s. 4

Proceeding continues where accused is fit

672.28 Where the verdict on trial of the issue is that an accused is fit to stand trial, the arraignment, preliminary inquiry, trial or other stage of the proceeding shall continue as if the issue of fitness of the accused had never arisen.

1991, c. 43, s. 4

Where continued detention in custody

672.29 Where an accused is detained in custody on delivery of a verdict that the accused is fit to stand trial, the court may order the accused to be detained in a hospital until the completion of the trial, if the court has reasonable grounds to believe that the accused would become unfit to stand trial if released.

1991, c. 43, s. 4

CASELAW

***R. v. Kurd*, [2005] O.J. No. 2794 (S.C.J.)**—It is not open to the hospital to return the accused to a detention centre while subject to an order pursuant to the provisions of section 672.29 of the *Criminal Code*.[88]

* * * * *

Acquittal

672.3 Where the court has postponed directing the trial of the issue of fitness of an accused pursuant to subsection 672.25(2) and the accused is discharged or acquitted before the issue is tried, it shall not be tried.

1991, c. 43, s. 4

Verdict of unfit to stand trial

672.31 Where the verdict on trial of the issue is that an accused is unfit to stand trial, any plea that has been made shall be set aside and any jury shall be discharged.

1991, c. 43, s. 4

Subsequent proceedings

672.32 (1) A verdict of unfit to stand trial shall not prevent the accused from being tried subsequently where the accused becomes fit to stand trial.

Burden of proof

(2) The burden of proof that the accused has subsequently become fit to stand trial is on the party who asserts it, and is discharged by proof on the balance of probabilities.

1991, c. 43, s. 4

***Prima facie* case to be made every two years**

672.33 (1) The court that has jurisdiction in respect of the offence charged against an accused who is found unfit to stand trial shall hold an inquiry, not later than two years after the verdict

88 *Ibid.*

is rendered and every two years thereafter until the accused is acquitted pursuant to subsection (6) or tried, to decide whether sufficient evidence can be adduced at that time to put the accused on trial.

CASELAW

***R. v. I. (J.)*, 2000 BCSC 175**—The accused's application for an order staying the proceedings was dismissed. The accused was a seventeen-year-old permanent Ward of the Minister with intellectual impairment, fetal alcohol syndrome, and epilepsy. He was found unfit to stand trial in relation to the charge of sexually assaulting a four-year-old child when he was a young person. The inquiry requested by the Crown into the accused's mental capacity under section 672.33 was mandatory.[89] The Youth Court did not lose jurisdiction because the accused was going to be an adult by the time the inquiry would be heard. The inquiry under section 672.33 goes to the issue of detention, rather than the issue of loss of jurisdiction.[90]

* * * * *

Extension of time for holding inquiry
(1.1) Despite subsection (1), the court may extend the period for holding an inquiry where it is satisfied on the basis of an application by the prosecutor or the accused that the extension is necessary for the proper administration of justice.

Court may order inquiry to be held
(2) On application of the accused, the court may order an inquiry under this section to be held at any time if it is satisfied, on the basis of the application and any written material submitted by the accused, that there is reason to doubt that there is a *prima facie* case against the accused.

Burden of proof
(3) At an inquiry under this section, the burden of proof that sufficient evidence can be adduced to put the accused on trial is on the prosecutor.

Admissible evidence at an inquiry
(4) In an inquiry under this section, the court shall admit as evidence
(a) any affidavit containing evidence that would be admissible if given by the person making the affidavit as a witness in court; or
(b) any certified copy of the oral testimony given at a previous inquiry or hearing held before a court in respect of the offence with which the accused is charged.

Conduct of inquiry
(5) The court may determine the manner in which an inquiry under this section is conducted and may follow the practices and procedures in respect of a preliminary inquiry under Part XVIII where it concludes that the interests of justice so require.

Where *prima facie* case not made
(6) Where, on the completion of an inquiry under this section, the court is satisfied that sufficient evidence cannot be adduced to put the accused on trial, the court shall acquit the accused.
1991, c. 43, s. 4; 2005, c. 22, ss. 13, 42(F)

* * * * *

89 *R. v. I. (J.)*, 2000 BCSC 175 at para. 15.
90 *Ibid.* at para. 31.

VERDICT OF NOT CRIMINALLY RESPONSIBLE ON ACCOUNT OF MENTAL DISORDER

Verdict of not criminally responsible on account of mental disorder
672.34 Where the jury, or the judge or provincial court judge where there is no jury, finds that an accused committed the act or made the omission that formed the basis of the offence charged, but was at the time suffering from mental disorder so as to be exempt from criminal responsibility by virtue of subsection 16(1), the jury or the judge shall render a verdict that the accused committed the act or made the omission but is not criminally responsible on account of mental disorder.
1991, c. 43, s. 4

CASELAW

THE JURISDICTION TO DETERMINE WHETHER THE ACCUSED IS NCRMD

***R. v. Café*, 2019 ONCA 775**—When the jury is discharged, jurisdiction to determine whether the accused is NCRMD does not pass from the jury to the trial judge. In these circumstances, a trial judge has no jurisdiction to interfere with the jury's verdict and the case must proceed to sentence. Any remedy that an accused person may have occurs on appeal.[91]

NO EVIDENCE OF INSANITY

***R. v. Charest*, [1990] Q.J. No. 405 (C.A.)**—Where, at the conclusion of the trial, the trial judge is of the view that there is no evidence to support the defence of insanity, the judge should inform counsel prior to their jury addresses. An accused may be found insane under the first arm of the test under section 16(2) where they suffer from a delusion of such intensity as to cause the act to take on a very different character in the mind of the accused.

JURY INSTRUCTIONS

***R. v. Goudreau*, 2019 ONCA 964**—When the jury asks if the accused is eligible for an insurance payout if found NCR, the jury should be instructed by the trial judge that it cannot consider the financial consequences of its verdict.

***R. v. Spence*, 2017 ONCA 619**—Even if a defence of NCRMD under section 16 is not advanced, the trial judge should provide jury instructions along these lines as it relates to intent if there is some evidence that the accused suffers from mental health issues. In this case, the trial judge's instructions on the *mens rea* for murder and how the appellant's mental health issues and claim of accident may negate that *mens rea* were confusing and contained errors.

***King, Re*, 2014 ONCA 76**—There was no error in the judge's explanation to the jury of the consequences of an NCR finding. Ample evidence supported the verdict of NCR. The explanation was a "natural corollary" to the evidence about the accused's mental condition prior to trial, his fitness to stand trial, and the role of the Ontario Review Board in determining that outcome.[92] The explanation avoided any misunderstanding that the result might be that the accused would

---

91 *R. v. Café*, 2019 ONCA 775 at para. 72, citing *R. v. Head*, [1986] 2 S.C.R. 684 at 698 and Joan Barrett & Riun Shandler, *Mental Disorder in Canadian Criminal Law* (Toronto: Thomson Reuters Canada, 2006, 2017) (loose-leaf updated 2018, release 4) at 4-44.3–4-44.7.

92 *King, Re*, 2014 ONCA 76 at para. 4.

be freed immediately without condition. The jury charge clearly told the jury not to consider the consequence of an NCR finding in reaching their decision and counsel did not object.

Note: ***King, Re*, 2014 ONCA 76** does not set out the exact explanation provided by the trial judge. At para. 4, the court noted that the concern about consequential reasoning if the jury is told about punishment—a concern raised in ***R. v. Latimer*, [1997] 1 S.C.R. 217**—is "somewhat muted with an NCR finding, which is a consequence rather than a punishment."

***R. v. Swain*, [1991] 1 S.C.R. 933**—If, during the course of a trial, the accused raises evidence of mental impairment which, in the view of the trial judge, puts mental capacity in issue, the Crown is entitled to lead evidence of insanity, and the trial judge is entitled to charge the jury in the defence of insanity within the meaning of section 16.

***R. v. Ratti*, [1991] 1 S.C.R. 68**—It is not an error for a trial judge to instruct the jury that "psychiatry, like any other branch of medicine, is not an exact science" and that "an individual judgment is always a factor in psychiatric assessments." It is correct to advise the jury to consider expert testimony in relation to the facts and that the testimony could be rejected if based upon factual assumptions with which the expert disagreed.

***R. v. Theriault*, [1981] 1 S.C.R. 336**—When expert evidence is adduced, it is the duty of counsel proffering such evidence to elicit from the expert translations of technical jargon into a comprehensible form for the jury. There is no obligation upon the trial judge to interpret the expert's testimony; indeed, such an undertaking is dangerous as it is susceptible to error. The trial judge may, in their charge to the jury, simplify or condense expert testimony, but failure to do so is not a fatal error.

* * * * *

Effect of verdict of not criminally responsible on account of mental disorder

672.35 Where a verdict of not criminally responsible on account of mental disorder is rendered, the accused shall not be found guilty or convicted of the offence, but

(a) the accused may plead *autrefois acquit* in respect of any subsequent charge relating to that offence;

(b) any court may take the verdict into account in considering an application for judicial interim release or in considering what dispositions to make or sentence to impose for any other offence; and

(c) the Parole Board of Canada or any provincial parole board may take the verdict into account in considering an application by the accused for parole or for a record suspension under the *Criminal Records Act* in respect of any other offence.

1991, c. 43, s. 4; 2012, c. 1, ss. 145, 160

Verdict not a previous conviction

672.36 A verdict of not criminally responsible on account of mental disorder is not a previous conviction for the purposes of any offence under any Act of Parliament for which a greater punishment is provided by reason of previous convictions.

1991, c. 43, s. 4

Definition of application for federal employment

672.37 (1) In this section, application for federal employment means an application form relating to

(a) employment in any department, as defined in section 2 of the *Financial Administration Act*;

(b) employment by any Crown corporation as defined in subsection 83(1) of the *Financial Administration Act*;

(c) enrolment in the Canadian Forces; or
(d) employment in connection with the operation of any work, undertaking or business that is within the legislative authority of Parliament.

Application for federal employment
(2) No application for federal employment shall contain any question that requires the applicant to disclose any charge or finding that the applicant committed an offence that resulted in a finding or a verdict of not criminally responsible on account of mental disorder if the applicant was discharged absolutely or is no longer subject to any disposition in respect of that offence.

Punishment
(3) Any person who uses or authorizes the use of an application for federal employment that contravenes subsection (2) is guilty of an offence punishable on summary conviction.
1991, c. 43, s. 4

Review Boards

Review Boards to be established
672.38 (1) A Review Board shall be established or designated for each province to make or review dispositions concerning any accused in respect of whom a verdict of not criminally responsible by reason of mental disorder or unfit to stand trial is rendered, and shall consist of not fewer than five members appointed by the lieutenant governor in council of the province.

Treated as provincial Board
(2) A Review Board shall be treated as having been established under the laws of the province.

Personal liability
(3) No member of a Review Board is personally liable for any act done in good faith in the exercise of the member's powers or the performance of the member's duties and functions or for any default or neglect in good faith in the exercise of those powers or the performance of those duties and functions.
1991, c. 43, s. 4; 1997, c. 18, s. 83

Members of Review Board
672.39 A Review Board must have at least one member who is entitled under the laws of a province to practise psychiatry and, where only one member is so entitled, at least one other member must have training and experience in the field of mental health, and be entitled under the laws of a province to practise medicine or psychology.
1991, c. 43, s. 4

Chairperson of a Review Board
672.4 (1) Subject to subsection (2), the chairperson of a Review Board shall be a judge of the Federal Court or of a superior, district or county court of a province, or a person who is qualified for appointment to, or has retired from, such a judicial office.

Transitional
(2) Where the chairperson of a Review Board that was established before the coming into force of subsection (1) is not a judge or other person referred to therein, the chairperson may continue to act until the expiration of his or her term of office if at least one other member of the Review Board is a judge or other person referred to in subsection (1) or is a member of the bar of the province.
1991, c. 43, s. 4

Quorum of Review Board

672.41 (1) Subject to subsection (2), the quorum of a Review Board is constituted by the chairperson, a member who is entitled under the laws of a province to practise psychiatry, and any other member.

Transitional

(2) Where the chairperson of a Review Board that was established before the coming into force of this section is not a judge or other person referred to in subsection 672.4(1), the quorum of the Review Board is constituted by the chairperson, a member who is entitled under the laws of a province to practise psychiatry, and a member who is a person referred to in that subsection or a member of the bar of the province.

1991, c. 43, s. 4

Majority vote

672.42 A decision of a majority of the members present and voting is the decision of a Review Board.

1991, c. 43, s. 4

Powers of Review Boards

672.43 At a hearing held by a Review Board to make a disposition or review a disposition in respect of an accused, the chairperson has all the powers that are conferred by sections 4 and 5 of the *Inquiries Act* on persons appointed as commissioners under Part I of that Act.

1991, c. 43, s. 4; 2005, c. 22, s. 42(F)

Rules of Review Board

672.44 (1) A Review Board may, subject to the approval of the lieutenant governor in council of the province, make rules providing for the practice and procedure before the Review Board.

Application and publication of rules

(2) The rules made by a Review Board under subsection (1) apply to any proceeding within its jurisdiction, and shall be published in the *Canada Gazette*.

Regulations

(3) Notwithstanding anything in this section, the Governor in Council may make regulations to provide for the practice and procedure before Review Boards, in particular to make the rules of Review Boards uniform, and all regulations made under this subsection prevail over any rules made under subsection (1).

1991, c. 43, s. 4

Disposition Hearings

Hearing to be held by a court

672.45 (1) Where a verdict of not criminally responsible on account of mental disorder or unfit to stand trial is rendered in respect of an accused, the court may of its own motion, and shall on application by the accused or the prosecutor, hold a disposition hearing.

Transmittal of transcript to Review Board

(1.1) If the court does not hold a hearing under subsection (1), it shall send without delay, following the verdict, in original or copied form, any transcript of the court proceedings in respect of the accused, any other document or information related to the proceedings, and all exhibits filed with it, to the Review Board that has jurisdiction in respect of the matter, if the transcript, document, information or exhibits are in its possession.

Disposition to be made

(2) At a disposition hearing, the court shall make a disposition in respect of the accused, if it is satisfied that it can readily do so and that a disposition should be made without delay.

1991, c. 43, s. 4; 2005, c. 22, ss. 14, 42(F)

Status quo pending Review Board hearing

672.46 (1) If the court does not make a disposition in respect of the accused at a disposition hearing, any order for the detention of the accused or any release order, appearance notice, summons or undertaking in respect of the accused that is in force at the time the verdict of not criminally responsible on account of mental disorder or unfit to stand trial is rendered continues in force, subject to its terms, until the Review Board makes a disposition.

Variation

(2) Despite subsection (1), a court may, pending a disposition by the Review Board in respect of the accused, on cause being shown, vacate the detention order, release order, appearance notice, summons or undertaking referred to in that subsection, and make any other order for the detention of the accused or any other release order that the court considers to be appropriate in the circumstances, including an order directing that the accused be detained in custody in a hospital.

1991, c. 43, s. 4; 2005, c. 22, s. 42(F); 2019, c. 25, s. 276

Review Board to make disposition where court does not

672.47 (1) Where a verdict of not criminally responsible on account of mental disorder or unfit to stand trial is rendered and the court makes no disposition in respect of an accused, the Review Board shall, as soon as is practicable but not later than forty-five days after the verdict was rendered, hold a hearing and make a disposition.

CASELAW

***Doucet v. British Columbia (Director of Adult Forensic Psychiatric Services)*, 2000 BCCA 195**—A valid order cannot be attacked in proceedings that do not focus on that order. Part XX.1 allows for procedural irregularities; failing to abide by the forty-five-day time limit without demonstrating substantial prejudice did not result in loss of jurisdiction. Parliament's intention was to permit late hearings unless the accused is prejudiced.

See also ***Martin v. British Columbia (Director of Adult Forensic Psychiatric Services) (sub nom. Martin, Re)*, 2000 CarswellBC 1226 (C.A.)**, leave to appeal to S.C.C. refused [2000] S.C.C.A. No. 412, 2001 CarswellBC 322—Where missing or failing to abide by a statutory time limit in section 672.81(1) causes no prejudice to the accused, the Board does not lose jurisdiction over the accused.

* * * * *

Extension of time for hearing

(2) Where the court is satisfied that there are exceptional circumstances that warrant it, the court may extend the time for holding a hearing under subsection (1) to a maximum of ninety days after the verdict was rendered.

Disposition made by court

(3) Where a court makes a disposition under section 672.54 other than an absolute discharge in respect of an accused, the Review Board shall, not later than ninety days after the disposition was made, hold a hearing and make a disposition in respect of the accused.

Exception—high-risk accused
(4) Despite subsections (1) to (3), if the court makes a disposition under subsection 672.64(3), the Review Board shall, not later than 45 days after the day on which the disposition is made, hold a hearing and make a disposition under paragraph 672.54(c), subject to the restrictions set out in that subsection.

Extension of time for hearing
(5) If the court is satisfied that there are exceptional circumstances that warrant it, the court may extend the time for holding a hearing under subsection (4) to a maximum of 90 days after the day on which the disposition is made.
1991, c. 43, s. 4; 2005, c. 22, ss. 15, 42(F); 2014, c. 6, s. 6

Review Board to determine fitness
672.48 (1) Where a Review Board holds a hearing to make or review a disposition in respect of an accused who has been found unfit to stand trial, it shall determine whether in its opinion the accused is fit to stand trial at the time of the hearing.

Review Board shall send accused to court
(2) If a Review Board determines that the accused is fit to stand trial, it shall order that the accused be sent back to court, and the court shall try the issue and render a verdict.

Chairperson may send accused to court
(3) The chairperson of a Review Board may, with the consent of the accused and the person in charge of the hospital where an accused is being detained, order that the accused be sent back to court for trial of the issue of whether the accused is unfit to stand trial, where the chairperson is of the opinion that
(a) the accused is fit to stand trial; and
(b) the Review Board will not hold a hearing to make or review a disposition in respect of the accused within a reasonable period.
1991, c. 43, s. 4; 2005, c. 22, s. 42(F)

CASELAW

***R. v. Pare* (2001), 159 C.C.C. (3d) 222 (Ont. C.A.)**—The Review Board's decision with respect to fitness to stand trial cannot be appealed.

* * * * *

Continued detention in hospital
672.49 (1) In a disposition made pursuant to section 672.47 the Review Board or chairperson may require the accused to continue to be detained in a hospital until the court determines whether the accused is fit to stand trial, if the Review Board or chairperson has reasonable grounds to believe that the accused would become unfit to stand trial if released.

CASELAW

***Evers v. British Columbia (Adult Forensic Psychiatric Services)*, 2009 BCCA 560**—The provisions of section **672.49** of the *Criminal Code* pertain only to initial hearings (s. 672.47). Accused, other than those at an initial hearing, maintain their disposition, which remains undisturbed by a Review Board's determination of fitness.[93]

* * * * *

Copy of disposition to be sent to court

(2) The Review Board or chairperson shall send a copy of a disposition made pursuant to section 672.47 without delay to the court having jurisdiction over the accused and to the Attorney General of the province where the accused is to be tried.

1991, c. 43, s. 4

Procedure at disposition hearing

672.5 (1) A hearing held by a court or Review Board to make or review a disposition in respect of an accused, including a hearing referred to in subsection 672.84(1) or (3), shall be held in accordance with this section.

Hearing to be informal

(2) The hearing may be conducted in as informal a manner as is appropriate in the circumstances.

Attorneys General may be parties

(3) On application, the court or Review Board shall designate as a party the Attorney General of the province where the disposition is to be made and, where an accused is transferred from another province, the Attorney General of the province from which the accused is transferred.

Interested person may be a party

(4) The court or Review Board may designate as a party any person who has a substantial interest in protecting the interests of the accused, if the court or Review Board is of the opinion that it is just to do so.

Notice of hearing

(5) Notice of the hearing shall be given to the parties, the Attorney General of the province where the disposition is to be made and, where the accused is transferred to another province, the Attorney General of the province from which the accused is transferred, within the time and in the manner prescribed, or within the time and in the manner fixed by the rules of the court or Review Board.

Notice

(5.1) At the victim's request, notice of the hearing and of the relevant provisions of the Act shall be given to the victim within the time and in the manner fixed by the rules of the court or Review Board.

Notice of discharge and intended place of residence

(5.2) If the accused is discharged absolutely under paragraph 672.54(a) or conditionally under paragraph 672.54(b), a notice of the discharge and accused's intended place of residence shall, at the victim's request, be given to the victim within the time and in the manner fixed by the rules of the court or Review Board.

Order excluding the public

(6) Where the court or Review Board considers it to be in the best interests of the accused and not contrary to the public interest, the court or Review Board may order the public or any members of the public to be excluded from the hearing or any part of the hearing.

---

93 Content reproduced with permission from *Fitness to Stand Trial*, above note 12 at Appendix A, 199.

CASELAW

***Blackman v. British Columbia Review Board*, [1995] B.C.J. No. 95 (C.A.)**—Section 672.5(6) of the *Criminal Code* violates neither section 7 nor 15 of the *Charter*. The NCR accused's application seeking exclusion of the media from his Review Board hearing was denied. The psychological stress arising from the media's presence did not affect the NCR accused's security as it did not rise to the level of having a severe and lasting impact.[94] The impugned provision did not discriminate against persons with mental disabilities.[95]

* * * * *

Right to counsel
(7) The accused or any other party has the right to be represented by counsel.

Assigning counsel
(8) If an accused is not represented by counsel, the court or Review Board shall, either before or at the time of the hearing, assign counsel to act for any accused
(a) who has been found unfit to stand trial; or
(b) wherever the interests of justice so require.

Counsel fees and disbursements
(8.1) Where counsel is assigned pursuant to subsection (8) and legal aid is not granted to the accused pursuant to a provincial legal aid program, the fees and disbursements of counsel shall be paid by the Attorney General to the extent that the accused is unable to pay them.

Taxation of fees and disbursements
(8.2) Where counsel and the Attorney General cannot agree on the fees or disbursements of counsel, the Attorney General or the counsel may apply to the registrar of the court and the registrar may tax the disputed fees and disbursements.

Right of accused to be present
(9) Subject to subsection (10), the accused has the right to be present during the whole of the hearing.

Removal or absence of accused
(10) The court or the chairperson of the Review Board may
(a) permit the accused to be absent during the whole or any part of the hearing on such conditions as the court or chairperson considers proper; or
(b) cause the accused to be removed and barred from re-entry for the whole or any part of the hearing
    (i) where the accused interrupts the hearing so that to continue in the presence of the accused would not be feasible,
    (ii) on being satisfied that failure to do so would likely endanger the life or safety of another person or would seriously impair the treatment or recovery of the accused, or
    (iii) in order to hear, in the absence of the accused, evidence, oral or written submissions, or the cross-examination of any witness concerning whether grounds exist for removing the accused pursuant to subparagraph (ii).

---

94 *Blackman v. British Columbia Review Board*, [1995] B.C.J. No. 95 at para. 60 (C.A.).

95 The s. 672.5(6) protections to the accused were not significantly different from those found in the *Corrections and Conditional Release Act* with respect to federal inmates seeking parole nor the *Young Offenders Act*, R.S.C. 1985, c. Y-1. Note that the *Young Offenders Act* was repealed in 2003 and replaced with the *Youth Criminal Justice Act*, S.C. 2002, c. 1.

CASELAW

APPLICATION

***Girard, Re*, 2016 ONCA 985**—Under section 672.5(10)(b)(i) of the *Criminal Code*, the Chair has the discretion to order the accused removed from the hearing "where the accused interrupts the hearing so that to continue in the presence of the accused would not be feasible." This power to exclude should be exercised exceedingly sparingly and only when there is no alternative. Patience and restraint should be exercised before resorting to the power to exclude.

*****

Rights of parties at hearing

(11) Any party may adduce evidence, make oral or written submissions, call witnesses and cross-examine any witness called by any other party and, on application, cross-examine any person who made an assessment report that was submitted to the court or Review Board in writing.

Request to compel attendance of witnesses

(12) A party may not compel the attendance of witnesses, but may request the court or the chairperson of the Review Board to do so.

Video links

(13) If the accused so agrees, the court or the chairperson of the Review Board may permit the accused to appear by closed-circuit television or videoconference for any part of the hearing.

CASELAW

NO AUTHORITY TO ORDER A VIDEOCONFERENCE REVIEW HEARING WITHOUT THE ACCUSED'S CONSENT

***R. v. Woods*, 2020 ONSC 6899, affirmed in *Woods, Re*, 2021 ONCA 190**—In the Superior Court case, the NCR accused did not provide her consent and objected to her annual review hearing proceeding by videoconference. After hearing from both parties with respect to whether the Board had jurisdiction to hold hearings by video without the consent of the NCRMD accused, the Ontario Review Board (ORB) ruled orally that it had authority to proceed with the review hearing by videoconference. The Superior Court found that the ORB exceeded its jurisdiction by ignoring the requirements of sections 672.5(9) and (13) of the *Criminal Code* and ordered the accused's personal appearance. The Board failed to consider whether it was possible to hold an in-person hearing, since there was no legal rule or public health recommendation preventing gatherings (of up to fifty persons). The applicant's request was mischaracterized by the ORB as her attempting to indefinitely adjourn her review hearing. The ORB also erred by holding a review hearing in the accused's absence, as she did not waive her right to be present. Parliament would need to amend section 672.5(13) of the *Code* to grant authority to the Board to order a videoconference review hearing without the consent of the accused. At para. 7 of the ONCA decision, the court dismissed the appeal and found "The Board did not have jurisdiction to proceed by videoconference without the consent of the NCR accused. It follows that the Board rendered Ms. Woods' 8 October 2020 disposition without jurisdiction. The disposition is therefore null and void for want of jurisdiction."[96]

---

96 **Note:** The Court of Appeal recognized that their interpretation of the law (i.e., leaving the decision as to whether a hearing will proceed via videoconference is up to the mentally disordered accused, since

Outside the NCR context, contrast the above case with ***R. v. Jefferies*, 2021 ONSC 1983**—Defence applications challenging an order for a remote trial, made without the accused's consent and made without an application from the Crown or the complainant, were dismissed. The trial judge had the jurisdiction to order a remote hearing over the objection of the accused and without an application being brought.

*****

Adjournment

(13.1) The Review Board may adjourn the hearing for a period not exceeding thirty days if necessary for the purpose of ensuring that relevant information is available to permit it to make or review a disposition or for any other sufficient reason.

Determination of mental condition of the accused

(13.2) On receiving an assessment report, the court or Review Board shall determine whether, since the last time the disposition in respect of the accused was made or reviewed there has been any change in the mental condition of the accused that may provide grounds for the discharge of the accused under paragraph 672.54(a) or (b) and, if there has been such a change, the court or Review Board shall notify every victim of the offence that they are entitled to file a statement in accordance with subsection (14).

Notice to victims—referral of finding to court

(13.3) If the Review Board refers to the court for review under subsection 672.84(1) a finding that an accused is a high-risk accused, it shall notify every victim of the offence that they are entitled to file a statement with the court in accordance with subsection (14).

Victim impact statement

(14) A victim of the offence may prepare and file with the court or Review Board a written statement describing the physical or emotional harm, property damage or economic loss suffered by the victim as the result of the commission of the offence and the impact of the offence on the victim. Form 48.2 in Part XXVIII, or a form approved by the lieutenant governor in council of the province in which the court or Review Board is exercising its jurisdiction, must be used for this purpose.

CASELAW

***Gajewski, Re*, 2020 ONCA 4**—The court found that there was no basis to grant the complainant leave to intervene in the accused's appeal from the Board's disposition; it would have been unfair to the appellant to do so (para. 31). As a member of the community, the complainant's concern that she was at risk was addressed by the Board pursuant to its mandate to determine if the appellant posed a significant threat to public safety (para. 35). It is the Crown's responsibility to speak for the community where there is a concern with respect to whether the Board has carried out its mandate effectively.

***Klem, Re*, 2016 ONCA 119**—Although the victim impact statements contained impermissible material that was inflammatory in nature, the Board's acceptance of the unredacted statements into evidence did not taint its disposition. At paras. 49–51, the court sets out that various options exist to address impermissible or inflammatory content in victim impact statements: (1) the

---

in-person hearings were not possible because of the COVID-19 pandemic) may lead to dangerous situations but that it was a problem to be solved by Parliament, rather than by the Ontario Review Board or the courts.

parties could request the Board to rule on the admissibility of comments on which counsel cannot agree; (2) the Board could direct counsel to attempt to agree on which portions of the victim impact statements should be redacted; or (3) the Board could admit a victim impact statement in full, while only taking into consideration those parts that comply with the *Criminal Code*.

***Agathos, Re*, 2009 Carswell Ont 9819, [2009] O.R.B.D. No. 1157 (Ont. Review Bd.)**—Where a victim impact statement is submitted during a Review Board hearing pursuant to section 672.5(14), the panel will only consider those parts of the statements that do not go beyond the parameters of describing "the harm done to, or loss suffered by, the victim arising from the commission of the offence."

* * * * *

Copy of statement

(15) The court or Review Board shall ensure that a copy of any statement filed in accordance with subsection (14) is provided to the accused or counsel for the accused, and the prosecutor, as soon as practicable after a verdict of not criminally responsible on account of mental disorder is rendered in respect of the offence.

Presentation of victim statement

(15.1) The court or Review Board shall, at the request of a victim, permit the victim to read a statement prepared and filed in accordance with subsection (14), or to present the statement in any other manner that the court or Review Board considers appropriate, unless the court or Review Board is of the opinion that the reading or presentation of the statement would interfere with the proper administration of justice.

Inquiry by court or Review Board

(15.2) The court or Review Board shall, as soon as practicable after a verdict of not criminally responsible on account of mental disorder is rendered in respect of an offence and before making a disposition under section 672.45, 672.47 or 672.64, inquire of the prosecutor or a victim of the offence, or any person representing a victim of the offence, whether the victim has been advised of the opportunity to prepare a statement referred to in subsection (14).

Adjournment

(15.3) On application of the prosecutor or a victim or of its own motion, the court or Review Board may adjourn the hearing held under section 672.45, 672.47 or 672.64 to permit the victim to prepare a statement referred to in subsection (14) if the court or Review Board is satisfied that the adjournment would not interfere with the proper administration of justice.

(16) [Repealed, 2015, c. 13, s. 22]

1991, c. 43, s. 4; 1997, c. 18, s. 84; 1999, c. 25, s. 11 (Preamble); 2005, c. 22, ss. 16, 42(F); 2014, c. 6, s. 7; 2015, c. 13, s. 22; 2019, c. 25, s. 277

Order restricting publication—sexual offences

672.501 (1) Where a Review Board holds a hearing referred to in section 672.5 in respect of an accused who has been declared not criminally responsible on account of mental disorder or unfit to stand trial for an offence referred to in subsection 486.4(1), the Review Board shall make an order directing that any information that could identify a victim, or a witness who is under the age of eighteen years, shall not be published in any document or broadcast or transmitted in any way.

Order restricting publication—child pornography

(2) Where a Review Board holds a hearing referred to in section 672.5 in respect of an accused who has been declared not criminally responsible on account of mental disorder or unfit to stand

trial for an offence referred to in section 163.1, a Review Board shall make an order directing that any information that could identify a witness who is under the age of eighteen years, or any person who is the subject of a representation, written material or a recording that constitutes child pornography within the meaning of section 163.1, shall not be published in any document or broadcast or transmitted in any way.

Order restricting publication—other offences

(3) Where a Review Board holds a hearing referred to in section 672.5 in respect of an accused who has been declared not criminally responsible on account of mental disorder or unfit to stand trial for an offence other than the offences referred to in subsection (1) or (2), on application of the prosecutor, a victim or a witness, the Review Board may make an order directing that any information that could identify the victim or witness shall not be published in any document or broadcast or transmitted in any way if the Review Board is satisfied that the order is necessary for the proper administration of justice.

Order restricting publication

(4) An order made under any of subsections (1) to (3) does not apply in respect of the disclosure of information in the course of the administration of justice if it is not the purpose of the disclosure to make the information known in the community.

Application and notice

(5) An applicant for an order under subsection (3) shall

(a) apply in writing to the Review Board; and

(b) provide notice of the application to the prosecutor, the accused and any other person affected by the order that the Review Board specifies.

Grounds

(6) An applicant for an order under subsection (3) shall set out the grounds on which the applicant relies to establish that the order is necessary for the proper administration of justice.

Hearing may be held

(7) The Review Board may hold a hearing to determine whether an order under subsection (3) should be made, and the hearing may be in private.

Factors to be considered

(8) In determining whether to make an order under subsection (3), the Review Board shall consider

(a) the right to a fair and public hearing;

(b) whether there is a real and substantial risk that the victim or witness would suffer significant harm if their identity were disclosed;

(c) whether the victim or witness needs the order for their security or to protect them from intimidation or retaliation;

(d) society's interest in encouraging the reporting of offences and the participation of victims and witnesses in the criminal justice process;

(e) whether effective alternatives are available to protect the identity of the victim or witness;

(f) the salutary and deleterious effects of the proposed order;

(g) the impact of the proposed order on the freedom of expression of those affected by it; and

(h) any other factor that the Review Board considers relevant.

Conditions

(9) An order made under subsection (3) may be subject to any conditions that the Review Board thinks fit.

Publication of application prohibited

(10) Unless the Review Board refuses to make an order under subsection (3), no person shall publish in any document or broadcast or transmit in any way

(a) the contents of an application;

(b) any evidence taken, information given or submissions made at a hearing under subsection (7); or

(c) any other information that could identify the person to whom the application relates as a victim or witness in the proceedings.

Offence

(11) Every person who fails to comply with an order made under any of subsections (1) to (3) is guilty of an offence punishable on summary conviction.

Application of order

(12) For greater certainty, an order referred to in subsection (11) also prohibits, in relation to proceedings taken against any person who fails to comply with the order, the publication in any document or the broadcasting or transmission in any way of information that could identify a victim or witness whose identity is protected by the order.

2005, c. 22, ss. 17, 64

Definition of disposition information

672.51 (1) In this section, disposition information means all or part of an assessment report submitted to the court or Review Board and any other written information before the court or Review Board about the accused that is relevant to making or reviewing a disposition.

Disposition information to be made available to parties

(2) Subject to this section, all disposition information shall be made available for inspection by, and the court or Review Board shall provide a copy of it to, each party and any counsel representing the accused.

Exception where disclosure dangerous to any person

(3) The court or Review Board shall withhold some or all of the disposition information from an accused where it is satisfied, on the basis of that information and the evidence or report of the medical practitioner responsible for the assessment or treatment of the accused, that disclosure of the information would be likely to endanger the life or safety of another person or would seriously impair the treatment or recovery of the accused.

Idem

(4) Notwithstanding subsection (3), the court or Review Board may release some or all of the disposition information to an accused where the interests of justice make disclosure essential in its opinion.

Exception where disclosure unnecessary or prejudicial

(5) The court or Review Board shall withhold disposition information from a party other than the accused or an Attorney General, where disclosure to that party, in the opinion of the court or Review Board, is not necessary to the proceeding and may be prejudicial to the accused.

Exclusion of certain persons from hearing

(6) A court or Review Board that withholds disposition information from the accused or any other party pursuant to subsection (3) or (5) shall exclude the accused or the other party, as the case may be, from the hearing during

(a) the oral presentation of that disposition information; or

(b) the questioning by the court or Review Board or the cross-examination of any person concerning that disposition information.

Prohibition of disclosure in certain cases

(7) No disposition information shall be made available for inspection or disclosed to any person who is not a party to the proceedings

(a) where the disposition information has been withheld from the accused or any other party pursuant to subsection (3) or (5); or

(b) where the court or Review Board is of the opinion that disclosure of the disposition information would be seriously prejudicial to the accused and that, in the circumstances, protection of the accused takes precedence over the public interest in disclosure.

Idem

(8) No part of the record of the proceedings in respect of which the accused was excluded pursuant to subparagraph 672.5(10)(b)(ii) or (iii) shall be made available for inspection to the accused or to any person who is not a party to the proceedings.

Information to be made available to specified persons

(9) Notwithstanding subsections (7) and (8), the court or Review Board may make any disposition information, or a copy of it, available on request to any person or member of a class of persons

(a) that has a valid interest in the information for research or statistical purposes, where the court or Review Board is satisfied that disclosure is in the public interest;

(b) that has a valid interest in the information for the purposes of the proper administration of justice; or

(c) that the accused requests or authorizes in writing to inspect it, where the court or Review Board is satisfied that the person will not disclose or give to the accused a copy of any disposition information withheld from the accused pursuant to subsection (3), or of any part of the record of proceedings referred to in subsection (8), or that the reasons for withholding that information from the accused no longer exist.

Disclosure for research or statistical purposes

(10) A person to whom the court or Review Board makes disposition information available under paragraph (9)(a) may disclose it for research or statistical purposes, but not in any form or manner that could reasonably be expected to identify any person to whom it relates.

Prohibition on publication

(11) No person shall publish in any document or broadcast or transmit in any way

(a) any disposition information that is prohibited from being disclosed pursuant to subsection (7); or

(b) any part of the record of the proceedings in respect of which the accused was excluded pursuant to subparagraph 672.5(10)(b)(ii) or (iii).

Powers of courts not limited

(12) Except as otherwise provided in this section, nothing in this section limits the powers that a court may exercise apart from this section.

1991, c. 43, s. 4; 1997, c. 18, s. 85; 2005, c. 22, ss. 18, 42(F), c. 32, s. 22; 2014, c. 6, s. 8

Record of proceedings

672.52 (1) The court or Review Board shall cause a record of the proceedings of its disposition hearings to be kept, and include in the record any assessment report submitted.

Transmittal of transcript to Review Board

(2) If a court holds a disposition hearing under subsection 672.45(1), whether or not it makes a disposition, it shall send without delay to the Review Board that has jurisdiction in respect of the matter, in original or copied form, a transcript of the hearing, any other document or information related to the hearing, and all exhibits filed with it, if the transcript, document, information or exhibits are in its possession.

Reasons for disposition and copies to be provided

(3) The court or Review Board shall state its reasons for making a disposition in the record of the proceedings, and shall provide every party with a copy of the disposition and those reasons.

1991, c. 43, s. 4; 2005, c. 22, ss. 19, 42(F)

Proceedings not invalid

672.53 Any procedural irregularity in relation to a disposition hearing does not affect the validity of the hearing unless it causes the accused substantial prejudice.

1991, c. 43, s. 4

DISPOSITIONS BY A COURT OR REVIEW BOARD

Terms of Dispositions

Dispositions that may be made

672.54 When a court or Review Board makes a disposition under subsection 672.45(2), section **672.47**, subsection 672.64(3) or section 672.83 or 672.84, it shall, taking into account the safety of the public, which is the paramount consideration, the mental condition of the accused, the reintegration of the accused into society and the other needs of the accused, make one of the following dispositions that is necessary and appropriate in the circumstances:

(a) where a verdict of not criminally responsible on account of mental disorder has been rendered in respect of the accused and, in the opinion of the court or Review Board, the accused is not a significant threat to the safety of the public, by order, direct that the accused be discharged absolutely;

(b) by order, direct that the accused be discharged subject to such conditions as the court or Review Board considers appropriate; or

(c) by order, direct that the accused be detained in custody in a hospital, subject to such conditions as the court or Review Board considers appropriate.

1991, c. 43, s. 4; 2005, c. 22, s. 20; 2014, c. 6, s. 9

CASELAW

EFFECT OF 2014 LEGISLATIVE AMENDMENT

***Ahmed-Hirse, Re*, 2014 CarswellOnt 10562, [2014] O.R.B.D. No. 1876 (Ont. Review Bd.)**—When the amendments to the wording of Part XX.1 of the *Criminal Code* came into effect on 30 July 2014, the current language of "necessary and appropriate" in section 672.54 did not change the requirement that the Board's disposition should be "the least onerous and least restrictive" (see paras. 34–36).

KEY OVERARCHING PRINCIPLES

***Valdez, Re*, 2018 ONCA 657**—The ease of returning an individual to hospital will not always justify a detention order as the necessary and appropriate disposition. There are multiple ways to secure a person's attendance at hospital when they fail to comply with a condition of their discharge:

(1) by convening a new hearing under section 672.82(1) of the *Criminal Code*; (2) by resorting to the breach provisions of the *Criminal Code*; or (3) through the committal provisions available under the *Mental Health Act*, R.S.O. 1990, c M.7.[97]

***R. v. Capano*, 2013 ONCA 737**—A need to supervise housing justifies a detention order as opposed to a discharge. This has been held by the Ontario Court of Appeal many times. See, for example, ***Brockville Psychiatric Hospital v. McGillis* (1996), 93 O.A.C. 226 (C.A.)**; ***Runnalls, Re*, 2012 ONCA 295**; ***Coburn, Re*, 2015 ONCA 186**; ***Ontario Shores Centre for Mental Health Sciences v. Boehme*, 2016 ONCA 706**; and ***Munezero, Re*, 2017 ONCA 585**.

***Mazzei v. British Columbia (Director of Adult Forensic Psychiatric Services)*, 2006 SCC 7**—At para. 7: "Review Boards have the power to bind hospital authorities and to impose binding conditions regarding or supervising (but not prescribing or imposing) medical treatment for an NCR accused." This jurisdiction arises from the wording within section 672.54, the legislative scheme, and Parliament's intention in enacting the law, as well as the relevant caselaw. The appropriate standard of review is correctness.[98] At para. 32: "[T]he primary purpose of the legislative scheme, is to protect the public while minimizing any restrictions on the NCR accused's liberty interests."

***Penetanguishene Mental Health Centre v. Ontario (Attorney General)*, 2004 SCC 20 (also referred to as *Tulikorpi*)**—The *Criminal Code* entitles the NCR accused to conditions that are the least onerous and least restrictive of the accused's liberty interest consistent with public safety, the accused's mental condition and "other needs," and eventual reintegration into society. The "least onerous and least restrictive" requirement applies not only to the choice between the three potential dispositions (i.e., absolute discharge, conditional discharge, or continued detention), but also to the conditions forming that disposition. The disposition and its conditions cannot be isolated from each other. The naming of a specific hospital or the type of hospital within which the accused is to be detained is not a condition but is instead an integral part of the disposition under section 672.54(c) of the *Criminal Code*.[99] See also this appeal's companion case, which was released concurrently, ***Pinet v. St. Thomas Psychiatric Hospital*, 2004 SCC 21**.

***Pinet v. St. Thomas Psychiatric Hospital*, 2004 SCC 21**—The court must consider whether the Ontario Review Board appropriately balanced the twin goals of public safety and fair treatment of the NCRMD accused. The liberty interest of the NCRMD accused must be taken into account at all stages of the Review Board's consideration, in accordance with the principles of fundamental justice. At para. 19:

> In this process of reconciliation, public safety is paramount. However, within the outer boundaries defined by public safety, the liberty interest of an NCR accused should be a major preoccupation of the Review Board when, taking into consideration public safety, the mental condition and other needs of the individual concerned, and his or her potential reintegration into society, it makes its disposition order.

The Ontario Review Board is required to craft a disposition complying with section 672.54 even with respect to transfer hearings pursuant to sections 672.54(b) and 672.54(c). Section 672.54 applies to conditions of detention, including the level of security. See also this appeal's companion case, which was released concurrently, ***Penetanguishene Mental Health Centre v. Ontario (Attorney General)*, 2004 SCC 20**.

---

97 *Valdez, Re*, 2018 ONCA 657 at para. 22 [*Valdez, Re*]. The court cites *Young, Re*, 2011 ONCA 432 at para. 26.

98 *Mazzei v. British Columbia (Director of Adult Forensic Psychiatric Services)*, 2006 SCC 7 at para. 16 [*Mazzei*].

99 *Penetanguishene Mental Health Centre v. Ontario (Attorney General)*, [2004] 1 S.C.R. 498 at paras. 39–40.

***Winko v. British Columbia (Forensic Psychiatric Institute)*, [1999] 2 S.C.R. 625**—If the NCR accused does not pose a significant threat to the safety of the public, then an absolute discharge must be ordered. To be a significant threat to the safety of the public, the threat must be: (1) more than speculative in nature and must be supported by the evidence; (2) significant, in the sense of there being a real risk of physical or psychological harm to individuals in the community and in the sense that this potential harm must be serious; and (3) the conduct creating the harm must be criminal in nature.[100]

KEY *CHARTER* CASES

***Winko v. British Columbia (Forensic Psychiatric Institute)*, [1999] 2 S.C.R. 625**—Part XX.1 (specifically, section 672.54) of the *Criminal Code* violates neither section 7 nor 15 of the *Charter*. The constitutionality of the scheme was saved by the requirement that "an absolute discharge be granted unless the court or Review Board is able to conclude that [the NCR accused persons] pose a significant risk to the safety of the public."[101] The purpose of Part XX.1 is based on the twin goals of fair treatment for those found NCRMD and public safety.

***R. v. LePage*, [1999] 2 S.C.R. 744**—Part XX.1 (specifically the disposition and review provisions) of the *Criminal Code* does not violate section 7 or 15 of the *Charter*. The provisions strike the appropriate balance between the accused's interest and public safety.

***R. v. Conway*, [2010] 1 S.C.R. 765**—The Review Board has the power to determine constitutional questions that arise at its hearings. However, remedies may only be those found within the limits of Part XX.1 of the *Criminal Code*.

JURISDICTION — GENERAL

***Aghdasi, Re*, 2011 ONCA 57**—Where the Court of Appeal finds that the appellant continues to be a significant threat to public safety despite recent progress, it does not have the power to reverse NCR findings and impose a sentence. In determining the least onerous disposition, the Board should consider factors such as: (1) whether linguistic and cultural isolation is interfering with community reintegration, and (2) whether the current facility meets the accused's current needs.

DUTY TO INQUIRE

***Murray, Re*, 2020 ONCA 547**—An obligation to inquire will arise where there is a foundation before the Board supporting the need for further investigation to ensure an appropriate disposition.[102] The duty is a unilateral one that falls on the Board. It is not dependent on a request for inquiry being made by a party before it.[103]

***R. v. LePage*, [2006] O.J. No. 4486 (C.A.)**—LePage languished for twenty-eight years, refusing treatment. The danger posed to the public remained unchanged and LePage was receiving no treatment because of his unwillingness to engage. In this case, it was unclear what might break the impasse or if the impasse could be broken, but after twenty-eight years, it was incumbent on the Board to consider making further inquiry. The Board's burden to search out and consider

---

100 *Winko v. British Columbia (Forensic Psychiatric Institute)*, [1999] 2 S.C.R. 625 at para. 57 [*Winko*].

101 *Ibid.* at para. 3.

102 *Murray, Re*, 2020 ONCA 547 at para. 17.

103 *Ibid.* at para. 18.

evidence extends to evidence favouring the restriction of the NCR accused as well as evidence in his favour, regardless of whether the NCR accused is present.[104]

APPLICATION — GLADUE REPORTS AND PRINCIPLES

***Cooper, Re*, 2024 ONCA 484** — The appellant — a 35-year-old Indigenous man who was found NCR with respect to a charge of assault causing bodily harm — successfully appealed the Ontario Review Board's refusal to order a Gladue Report for the next annual hearing. A Gladue Report was relevant to the attending psychiatrist's suggestion that intergenerational trauma might exist in the appellant's family and that such a report might be helpful in assisting with treatment. It was unnecessary and unreasonable for the Board to delay the preparation of the Gladue Report.

***Summers, Re*, 2024 ONCA 772** — The Board determined that the accused continued to pose a significant risk of serious harms to others because of his treatment-resistant psychosis and substance use disorder. The least onerous and restrictive disposition was detention with specified privileges. Gladue principles were considered and respected in the Board's analysis. The accused failed to adhere to his medication regime, despite efforts to facilitate family visits and introduce the accused to Indigenous supports and programming. The Court set out the requirements on the Board in properly applying *Gladue* principles to aboriginal NCR accused persons at para. 18:

> The proper application of *Gladue* principles will not always lead to a different disposition as compared to a non-Indigenous person. What is required is that the Board be alert — at each stage of the analysis — to the potential to overlook "the unique circumstances of aboriginal NCR accused and ensure that it has adequate information in relation to the aboriginal background of an NCR accused to enable the ORB to assess the reintegration of the accused into society and the accused's other needs ...": *R. v. Sim* (2005), 78 O.R. (3d) 183 (C.A.), at para. 29.

APPLICATION — PRINCIPLES RELATED TO DETENTION BEING THE LEAST ONEROUS AND RESTRICTIVE DISPOSITION

***Lamb, Re*, 2014 ONCA 169**—When an accused who poses a significant threat to the safety of the public is incapable of consenting to treatment, a conditional discharge is not an option. In this particular case, a detention order was the least onerous and restrictive option based on the evidence.

APPLICATION—PRINCIPLES RELATED TO CONDITIONAL DISCHARGES

***Dhanpaul, Re*, 2024 ONCA 170** — The Board's decision to impose a conditional discharge was reasonable based on the evidence. The appellant continued to pose a significant threat to public safety given the appellant's ongoing psychotic symptoms, limited insight into his illness, intention to leave the support facility, and expert opinion evidence that the appellant was at a high risk of recidivism and aggressive behaviour without supervision as the appellant would very likely drift away from community supports and stop taking medication.

***R. v. Scalabrini*, 2021 ONCA 212**—The need for the mental health facility to approve of the appellant's accommodation and the need to intervene early in the event of decompensation are entirely appropriate factors for consideration in rejecting a conditional discharge.[105]

---

104 *LePage* (C.A.), above note 85 at para. 22.

105 *R. v. Scalabrini*, 2021 ONCA 212 at para. 22, citing *Jackson, Re*, 2018 ONCA 560 at para. 7; *Munezero, Re*, 2017 ONCA 585 at para. 9; *Ontario Shores Centre for Mental Health Sciences v. Boehme*, 2016 ONCA 706 at paras. 9–11.

***Valdez, Re*, 2018 ONCA 657**—"The Board has a duty to assess the evidentiary record in context, including taking into consideration in this case: (1) the risk of non-attendance for medication; (2) the mechanisms for securing someone's attendance at hospital under the conditional discharge framework; (3) the length of time that any such steps may take; (4) the effect of that delay on Mr. Valdez's mental health; and (5) the risk to public safety posed by any delay in treatment."[106]

***Marzec, Re*, 2015 ONCA 658**—The Board is not permitted to order a conditional discharge out of an abundance of caution. That is not the legal test. An absolute discharge must be ordered if the accused no longer poses a significant risk to the public. In this case, the Board erroneously placed the onus on the appellant to prove that he was not a risk before he was entitled to an absolute discharge.

***R. v. Breitwieser*, 2009 ONCA 784**[107]—In any case where the primary issue is compliance with conditions and there is an air of reality to the claim that a conditional discharge would be an appropriate disposition, the Board must address two elements: (1) the Board must canvass whether the accused will consent to the appropriate conditions under section 672.55 of the *Criminal Code*; and (2) the Board must address the potential mechanisms for the accused's return to the hospital in the event of non-compliance and determine whether the patient is likely to agree to return or whether a combination of section 672.55 and either section 672.92 or 672.93(2) or another route of return would be sufficient in the circumstances.[108]

***Brockville Psychiatric Hospital v. McGillis*, [1996] O.J. No. 3430 (C.A.)**—A conditional discharge under section 672.54(b) and a detention order under section 672.54(c) are two separate orders. A hybrid of these two orders is not permitted by the statutory scheme in Part XX.I of the *Criminal Code*. See also ***British Columbia (Forensic Psychiatric Institute) v. Johnson* (1995), 66 B.C.A.C. 34 at paras. 48–49 (C.A.)**. Distinguished in ***Lovell, Re*, 2015 CarswellOnt 18628**.

APPLICATION—PRINCIPLES RELATED TO ABSOLUTE DISCHARGES

***Smith, Re*, 2023 ONCA 468** — The NCR accused was discharged absolutely by a majority of the Ontario Review Board, which properly considered the relevant factors. The ORB reasonably concluded that the accused was not a significant threat to public safety and that his roommate was suitable to act as an external control. With respect to the roommate, the majority found the individual was a suitable external control because of her knowledge and training in the mental health field, her willingness to engage the Mental Health Act, and her living with the accused.

***Sim, Re*, 2020 ONCA 563**—The NCR accused was discharged absolutely after the Court of Appeal found that, with respect to the significant risk analysis, the Review Board failed to "analyze the likely occurrence of each of the steps in Dr. Gulati's cascading risk scenario having regard to all the evidence."[109] The Board's disposition continuing the appellant's conditional discharge was unreasonable. The Board simply accepted that the appellant's cannabis consumption would inevitably give rise to a substantial risk of serious harm to the public, requiring the appellant to remain on a disposition to protect the public. At para. 69: "The Board's analysis does not meet the *Vavilov* standard of justification, transparency and intelligibility and it is unreasonable."

---

106 *Valdez, Re*, above note 97 at para. 23.

107 In this particular case, the appellant was responsible for administering his own medication and, if the appellant failed to take his medication, he would quickly decompensate.

108 *R. v. Breitwieser*, 2009 ONCA 784 at para. 18.

109 *Sim, Re*, 2020 ONCA 563 at para. 97.

***Wall, Re*, 2017 ONCA 713**—Concerns of recent deterioration, where at its height marijuana use was *potentially* linked to *problematic symptoms*, are insufficient to support a finding of a significant threat and form an unreasonable basis on which to order continued detention in the face of the NCR accused's request for an absolute discharge. The Board had also rejected the expert evidence that the appellant was "extremely dangerous"; this was the only expert evidence presented.[110] The NCR accused is entitled to liberty absent a reasonable finding that the NCR accused poses a significant threat to the safety of the public.

***Capano, Re*, 2012 ONCA 172**—An accused found NCR on account of mental disorder and who fails to comply with the terms of a conditional discharge is not entitled to an absolute discharge where they continue to pose a significant threat to public safety. A detention order may be the least onerous and least restrictive disposition in such a case.

***Re Ferguson*, 2010 ONCA 810** —Whether an absolute discharge is in the appellant's best interests is not relevant to the Board's duty. The accused is entitled to liberty absent a reasonable finding that they pose a significant threat to the safety of the public.[111]

***Ontario Shores Centre for Mental Health Sciences v. Darch*, 2010 ONCA 36**—The Court of Appeal found the Board's decision to absolutely discharge the accused to be reasonable. The Board was alive to concerns expressed by some members of the NCR accused's medical team regarding possible public safety risk. The Board considered all of the evidence and could not say with any certainty that the accused was a risk to the public. The evidence before the Board at its highest was that the accused potentially could act violently if he stopped taking his medication, ceased living at his group home, lost his community supports, and resumed the use of cannabis. None of these speculative factors applied at the time of the Board hearing.[112]

***R. v. Owen*, 2003 SCC 33**—An absolute discharge with respect to an NCR accused should only be granted after considering all of the reliable evidence available at the time of the Board hearing and, if appealed, at the time of appellate review. In general, it is desirable for an appellate court to admit fresh evidence that is trustworthy and touches on the issue of risk to public safety as being necessary in the interests of justice.[113]

***Winko v. British Columbia (Forensic Psychiatric Institute)*, [1999] 2 S.C.R. 625**—If the NCR accused does not pose a significant threat to the safety of the public, then an absolute discharge must be ordered. To be a significant threat to the safety of the public, the threat must be: (1) more than speculative in nature and must be supported by the evidence; (2) significant, in the sense of there being a real risk of physical or psychological harm to individuals in the community and in the sense that this potential harm must be serious; and (3) the conduct creating the harm must be criminal in nature.[114]

APPLICATION—RISK ASSESSMENT TOOLS

***Ewert v. Canada*, 2018 SCC 30**—Correctional Services of Canada (CSC) did not breach the section 7 or 15 *Charter* rights of the appellant—a Métis federal inmate—by relying on psychological and risk assessment tools without ensuring they were valid when applied to Indigenous offenders. The tools were used to conduct needs and risks assessments. The CSC had knowledge of long-standing cultural bias concerns with respect to the application of these tools to Indigenous

110 *Wall, Re*, 2017 ONCA 713 at paras. 23–25 and 29 [*Wall*].

111 See also *Wall, ibid.* at para. 30 to the end.

112 *Ontario Shores Centre for Mental Health Sciences v. Darch*, 2010 ONCA 36 at paras. 20–21 [*Darch*].

113 *R. v. Owen*, 2003 SCC 33 at paras. 59 and 71 [*Owen*].

114 *Winko*, above note 100 at para. 57.

offenders. The CSC breached section 24(1) of the *Corrections and Conditional Release Act* (CCRA) by continuing to rely on these tools without ensuring their validity when applied to Indigenous offenders. With respect to section 7, the uncertainty with respect to the tests' accuracy when applied to Indigenous offenders did not establish arbitrariness or overbreadth. With respect to section 15, the evidence at trial established that there was a risk that the tools were less accurate when applied to Indigenous inmates (compared to non-Indigenous inmates) but the evidence did not establish the tools actually overestimated risk, led to harsher incarceration conditions, or to the denial of rehabilitative opportunities.[115]

***Krivicic, Re*, 2018 ONCA 535**—Results of risk assessment tools, such as the HCR-20V3 used in this case, are only capable of feeding into half of the equation mandated by section 672.54. As per *Winko*, section 672.54 requires an inquiry into: (1) the likelihood of the risk of reoffending and (2) the seriousness or magnitude of that offending. The HCR-20V3 says nothing about the second aspect of this inquiry.[116] In this case, the court concluded that the Board's conclusions were speculative.

***R. v. Simpson*, 2010 ONCA 302**—The expert opinion before the Board included evidence that approved accommodation was an important risk management tool. In such circumstances, the continued detention of the patient should be ordered.[117]

APPLICATION—RISK MANAGEMENT CONSIDERATIONS

***Piscopo, Re*, 2014 ONCA 19**—The Board made no error in finding that a detention order was the least onerous and least restrictive order that could be made for the accused at this time. The treating psychiatrist made it clear at the hearing that if the NCR accused were to stop taking his medication and decompensate, the methods for apprehending him under the *Criminal Code* or under the *Mental Health Act* would be insufficient to return him to hospital quickly enough to address his condition.

***Palmer, Re*, 2013 ONCA 475**—The accused was found NCR with respect to second-degree murder and was moved to a general forensic unit where he had community living privileges and lived in a co-ed unit without issue. The accused's progress stalled when he was charged with the sexual assault of an eighteen-year-old female co-patient, for which he was acquitted at trial. The Ontario Review Board ordered that the accused be transferred to a medium secure all-male unit at Brockville Mental Health Centre. The Court of Appeal dismissed the appeals of the accused and Brockville. The Board was entitled to use the facts surrounding the allegation to decide upon the least onerous and least restrictive disposition, despite the acquittal. There is no formal bar to the Board making use of the undisputed information that the accused purchased and used alcohol to excess in violation of his conditions and engaged in several sexual acts with a vulnerable eighteen-year-old patient.[118]

---

115 The challenged tools were the Hare Psychopathy Checklist-Revised (PCL-R); the Violence Risk Appraisal Guide (VRAG); the Sex Offender Risk Appraisal Guide (SORAG); the Static-99; and the Violence Risk Scale—Sex Offender (VRS-SO). Section 24(1) of the CCRA requires the CSC to "take all reasonable steps to ensure that any information about an offender that it uses is accurate, up to date and complete as possible."

116 *Krivicic, Re*, 2018 ONCA 535 at para. 60. Trotter J.A. cites that *R. v. Montgrand*, 2017 SKCA 49 at paras. 14–20 should be seen for a discussion of the limits of risk prediction assessments in the context of dangerous offender applications.

117 *R. v. Simpson*, 2010 ONCA 302 at para. 4. The case also recommends seeing the following cases: *Brockville Psychiatric Hospital v. McGillis*, [1996] O.J. No. 3430 at para. 4 (C.A.) and *Capano v. R.*, [2008] O.J. No. 1712 at para. 8 (C.A.).

118 *Palmer, Re*, 2013 ONCA 475 at paras. 31–33.

***Penetanguishene Mental Health Centre v. Magee*, [2006] O.J. No. 1926 (C.A.)**—Once the Review Board concludes that the NCR accused is a significant threat to the safety of the public, the Board must consider all factors in section 672.54, including the "least onerous and least restrictive" requirement. The issue is not simply identifying the lowest level of security at a hospital that could contain the risk posed by the NCR accused.[119] The Board's inquiry should not focus on the issue of risk management to the virtual exclusion of any meaningful consideration of the section 672.54 factors.[120] The core of the Review Board's analysis in this case was the NCR accused's "incapacitation" or "warehousing" to contain the NCR accused's risk; concern was not paid to the accused's treatment or liberty interests.[121]

APPLICATION—IMPOSING APPROPRIATE CONDITIONS

***Anderson, Re*, 2020 ONCA 277**—It is not necessary for the Board to have direct evidence amounting to an absolute certainty to impose a condition that is necessary in the specific circumstances of an individual's case. It would be contrary to the Board's duty to protect public safety if it were required to withhold from imposing a condition until an actual adverse event took place.

***Kachkar, Re*, 2014 ONCA 250**—The circumstances of the case involved the Crown arguing that the Board denied the Crown procedural fairness by imposing an additional community access condition as part of its disposition without allowing the Crown prior opportunity to make submissions. The Board does not owe a common law duty of procedural fairness to the Crown. The Crown is not an individual nor does it have a right, privilege, or interest affected by the Board's disposition. What was being asserted by the Crown is the public—rather than private—interest, which is contrasted with the respondent's liberty interest. The Board must ensure that its disposition is the least onerous and least restrictive to the accused while protecting public safety.

***R. v. Everingham*, 2014 ONCA 743**—An NCR offender has a significantly diminished expectation of privacy under Part XX.1 of the *Criminal Code*. The Ontario Review Board ordering the detention of the accused at a secure forensic psychiatric facility ("hospital") with the condition that the accused refrain from computer use unless he permitted staff to monitor such use did not offend the accused's rights under the *Mental Health Act* or section 8 of the *Charter*.

***Elster, Re*, 2011 ONCA 701** — The Board unilaterally included a term for supervised accommodation without hearing counsel on the issue, resulting in a denial of procedural fairness. In contrast, see *Abdikarim, Re*, 2024 ONCA 17, where the Court found that including a supervised accommodation requirement was appropriate; note that a Board member had raised the issue of supervised accommodation during the testimony of the staff psychiatrist, counsel were invited to ask questions of the staff psychiatrist on the subject, and counsel addressed supervised accommodation in closing submissions.

***Sim v. Ontario (Review Board)* (2005), 201 C.C.C. (3d) 482 (Ont. C.A.)**—In addition to the Review Board's obligation to ensure that sufficient evidence was being provided in order to address the criteria in section 672.54, the board had a duty to ensure that it had adequate evidence information regarding the accused's Aboriginal background where relevant to its determination of the least onerous and least restrictive disposition.

119 *Penetanguishene Mental Health Centre v. Magee*, [2006] O.J. No. 1926 at para. 64 (C.A.).
120 *Ibid.* at para. 65.
121 *Ibid.* at para. 67.

APPLICATION — ACCEPTANCE OF HEARSAY EVIDENCE

***Jaeger, Re*, 2016 ONCA 111** — The Board has wide latitude to accept hearsay evidence. An email from a hospital, submitted to ensure the completeness and accuracy of the record, is admissible.

***R. v. Vancurenko*, [2006] O.J. No. 2569 (C.A.)** — The Board "enjoys a wide latitude to receive hearsay evidence" as it is primarily inquisitorial rather than adversarial in nature (para. 2). The Board is entitled to receive, as in this case, a police summary of prior criminal activity at a review hearing. At para. 2, the court observed that "much of the evidence received by the Board in its hearings is in the nature of hearsay evidence." For similar findings on this issue, see also ***Ranieri, Re*, 2015 ONCA 444 at paras. 16–17; *Jaeger, Re*, 2016 ONCA 111 at para. 5; *R. v. Wodajio*, 2005 ABCA 45 at para. 33.**

APPLICATION — DRUG USE AND NON-COMPLIANCE WITH MEDICATION

***Sokal, Re*, 2018 ONCA 113** — The NCR accused's appeal from an order continuing his conditional discharge was allowed. The NCR accused had been living in the community independently since 2014 on conditions that included abstaining from drugs and alcohol. The accused used drugs twice in the eighteen months prior to the disposition.[122] The Board erred in concluding that the NCR accused posed a significant risk because of these two incidents of drug use given evidence of the NCR accused's medication compliance, lack of violence and aggression, ten-month drug-free period, admission to the Hamilton Program for Schizophrenia, and a lack of psychotic symptoms associated with recent drug use.[123]

***Wall, Re*, 2017 ONCA 713** — Concerns of recent deterioration, where at its height marijuana use was *potentially* linked to *problematic symptoms*, are insufficient to support a finding of a significant threat and form an unreasonable basis on which to order continued detention in the face of the NCR accused's request for an absolute discharge. The Board had also rejected the expert evidence that the appellant was "extremely dangerous"; this was the only expert evidence presented.[124] The NCR accused is entitled to liberty absent a reasonable finding that the NCR accused poses a significant threat to the safety of the public.

***Pellett, Re*, 2017 ONCA 753** — Evidence of non-compliance with medication should not be improperly extrapolated by the Board to support its conclusion that the appellant poses a significant threat to the safety of the public when there is otherwise insufficient evidence to support that finding. Whether the appellant would act out in a way contemplated by section 672.54 was purely speculative. In this case, the index offence appeared to be a "one-off incident."[125]

***Katzav, Re*, 2013 ONCA 627** — The Review Board's need to control the appellant's place of residence, a crucial factor in his ongoing management in the community, was sufficient to render a detention order the "least onerous and least restrictive" disposition available. It is problematic, however, for the Board to view a detention order as enhancing the possibility that the appellant will agree to take anti-psychotic medication. The appellant is entitled and able to make up his own mind about taking medication and restrictions on his liberty are not an appropriate means to encourage compliance with medication. In this case, this error had no effect on the Review Board's decision as the detention order was fully justified on the basis that it was necessary to give the hospital control over the appellant's housing. See paras. 28–29.

---

122 *Sokal, Re*, 2018 ONCA 113 at para. 24.

123 *Ibid.* at paras. 25–26.

124 *Wall*, above note 110 at paras. 23–25 and 29.

125 *Pellett, Re*, 2017 ONCA 753 at para. 30.

***Centre for Addiction and Mental Health v. R.*, 2010 ONCA 695**—It is unreasonable for the Board to grant an absolute discharge without addressing the issue of criminal history and without there being a proper plan to monitor the accused's condition. Where the decision of the Board is based upon there being certainty that the accused is medication compliant by virtue of reporting for injections, fresh evidence on appeal setting out a change to an oral prescription (i.e., non-reporting situation) may require that the Board's decision be set aside.

TRANSFERS

***Keizer, Re*, 2016 ONCA 483**—The Board denied the accused's request for an absolute discharge and ordered him to be transferred from a mental health centre to a hospital. The Board did not breach its duty of fairness by overriding the hospital's objection to the accused's transfer. The hospital was given notice of the transfer (pursuant to rule 13) and could have made submissions but chose not to and did not participate in the review process. The Board's transfer decision was reasonable.

***Armstrong, Re*, 2015 ONCA 326**—The Ontario Review Board's (ORB) disposition was that the accused could not be transferred from the Medium Secure Unit to the General Unit. The accused appealed the ORB's disposition. The application was dismissed by the Ontario Court of Appeal. The NCRMD accused attended programs but did not participate in them and the appellate court found that the Review Board's disposition not to transfer him from the Medium Secure Unit to the General Unit was reasonable, even when considering that the accused had no violent incidents and made some progress over the past year. The Board's findings that the accused refused treatment was reasonable and based on the evidence. The NCR accused was not receiving treatment and he was still demonstrating delusions and inappropriate behaviour. He was unable to progress to a less restrictive situation.

The above case is distinguished by ***Gonzalez, Re*, 2017 ONCA 102**.

***Conway, Re*, 2012 ONCA 519**—If a hospital transfer amounts to virtual segregation and is not the least onerous and least restrictive disposition, then the detention is nonetheless lawful if the measures taken by the hospital are reasonable in light of the dangerous conduct of the accused.

***MacLean, Re*, 2012 ONCA 909**—Paradoxically, a transfer from a general ward to a secure ward could constitute the least restrictive disposition where the more favourable staff-to-patient ratio in the secure setting provides the accused—who requires "close observation"—more objective freedom (para. 11).

***Hassan, Re*, 2011 ONCA 561**—Transfer from a minimum-security hospital unit to a medium-security hospital unit may indeed be the least onerous and least restrictive disposition in the face of decompensating behaviour that is of a different order of dangerousness compared to previous decompensating behaviour (which could still be maintained in a minimum secure unit). The Board should ideally explicitly address how recent decompensating behaviour leading to a more restrictive disposition is more dangerous than previous decompensating behaviour.

JOINT SUBMISSIONS

***Thurston, Re*, 2015 ONCA 351** —Automatically accepting a joint submission is inconsistent with the Board's statutory mandate. See para. 43. See also ***Osawe, Re*, 2015 ONCA 280 at paras. 33 and 57** as well as ***Hassan, Re*, 2011 ONCA 561 at para. 25**.

***O'Donnell, Re*, 2015 ONCA 882**—The Board has an inquisitorial mandate that can require it to look beyond the joint position of the parties. There is, however, no obligation for the Board to make any further inquiries.

REJECTING JOINT SUBMISSIONS

***Benjamin, Re*, 2016 ONCA 118**—The context of the matter and what occurred at the hearing can indicate the proposed disposition will not be easily accepted by the Board and must be amply demonstrated on the evidence. Questions asked by the Review Board panel that reflect reservations to continue with the original disposition is sufficient notice of its intention not to accept the joint submission, particularly when the unfit accused responds to the questions by calling evidence. It is preferable, however, that the Chair state from the outset the panel's reservations about continuing the original disposition.

***Osawe, Re*, 2015 ONCA 280**—The Board has the duty to reject a joint submission that does not meet the requirements of section 672.54. Procedural fairness must be afforded to all parties. The form of notice may vary but the objective of allowing the accused a meaningful opportunity to present the evidence and argument relevant to the Board's disposition must be satisfied. See para. 73 for acceptable methods of notice.

*****

Significant threat to safety of public

672.5401 For the purposes of section 672.54, a significant threat to the safety of the public means a risk of serious physical or psychological harm to members of the public—including any victim of or witness to the offence, or any person under the age of 18 years—resulting from conduct that is criminal in nature but not necessarily violent.

2014, c. 6, s. 10

CASELAW

THE STANDARD ITSELF: SIGNIFICANT THREAT TO THE SAFETY OF THE PUBLIC

***Wall, Re*, 2017 ONCA 713**—Concerns of recent deterioration, where at its height marijuana use was *potentially* linked to *problematic symptoms*, are insufficient to support a finding of a significant threat and form an unreasonable basis on which to order continued detention in the face of the NCR accused's request for an absolute discharge. The Board had also rejected the expert evidence that the appellant was "extremely dangerous"; this was the only expert evidence presented.[126] The NCR accused is entitled to liberty absent a reasonable finding that the NCR accused poses a significant threat to the safety of the public.

***Carrick, Re*, 2015 ONCA 866**—The "significant threat" standard is an onerous one. The Review Board must assess whether the NCR accused remains a "significant threat to the safety of the public"—this is the paramount consideration. There must be both a likelihood of a risk materializing and the likelihood that serious harm will occur. An NCR accused is not to be detained based on mere speculation. The Board must be satisfied as to both the existence and gravity of the risk of physical or psychological harm posed by the appellant to deny them an absolute discharge.

126 *Wall*, above note 110 at paras. 23–25 and 29.

***R. v. Ferguson*, 2010 ONCA 810**—The phrase "significant threat to the safety of the public" refers to:

> [A] foreseeable and substantial risk of physical or psychological harm to members of the public that is serious and beyond the trivial or annoying. A very small risk of even grave harm will not suffice. A high risk of relatively trivial harm will also not meet the substantial harm standard. While the conduct must be criminal in nature, not all criminal conduct will suffice to establish a substantial risk. There must be a risk that the NCR accused will commit a "serious criminal offence."[127]

***Winko v. British Columbia (Forensic Psychiatric Institute)*, [1999] 2 S.C.R. 625**—If the NCR accused does not pose a significant threat to the safety of the public, then an absolute discharge must be ordered. To be a significant threat to the safety of the public, the threat must be: (1) more than speculative in nature and must be supported by the evidence; (2) significant, in the sense of there being a real risk of physical or psychological harm to individuals in the community and in the sense that this potential harm must be serious; and (3) the conduct creating the harm must be criminal in nature.[128]

APPLICATION—IN GENERAL

***Viola, Re*, 2025 ONCA 33** – The finding that the NCR accused poses a significant threat to the safety of the public is a high threshold and the Review Board must be able to specify in its reasons the parts of the evidence that supports such a finding. In this case, the accused was NCR with respect to charges of robbery, assault, break and enter and mischief. The acts that led to the offences occurred while the accused experienced an "extremely unusual and acute medical event".129 The ORB imposed a detention order on the basis of the hospital report and the doctor's opinion that the NCR accused posed a threat to the safety of the public. The ORB failed to specify in its reasons what parts of either piece of evidence would support its finding that the accused posed a significant threat to the safety of the public. Indeed, the Board did "not identify anywhere in its reasons what evidence there was that could satisfy this high threshold."130 The NCR accused's appeal from a detention order was granted and an absolute discharge was granted.

***Kassa, Re*, 2019 ONCA 313**—As *Winko* instructs, there must be a "real" risk of physical or psychological harm arising from the criminal conduct. The Board failed to engage in the core analysis required by *Winko* by considering that there was a serious likelihood that the appellant's conduct *could* result in significant harm. "Could" does not suggest the "real" risk required by *Winko*.[131]

***Kalra, Re*, 2018 ONCA 833**—When assessing the likelihood of physical or psychological harm occurring from criminal conduct and the seriousness of the potential harm if the appellant is granted an absolute discharge, the Board must weigh the seriousness of the potential harm against the risk of that harm materializing.[132] Lack of insight is not of itself a basis to deny an absolute discharge. Insight is a treatment goal that some persons with mental illness may be unable to achieve. Whether an NCR accused has insight into their mental illness—and the extent of that insight—is only part of the significant threat to the safety of the public analysis.[133]

---

127 *R. v. Ferguson*, 2010 ONCA 810 at para. 8.
128 *Winko*, above note 100 at para. 57.
129 *Viola, Re*, 2025 ONCA 33 at para. 2.
130 *Ibid.* at para. 14.
131 *Kassa, Re*, 2019 ONCA 313 at paras. 33–36.
132 *Kalra, Re*, 2018 ONCA 833 at para. 51.
133 *Ibid.* at para. 52.

***Re Medcof*, 2018 ONCA 299**—It is not unreasonable for the Board to rely on the NCR accused's history of violence as part of its assessment of the expert evidence:[134] "While the conduct must be criminal in nature, not all criminal conduct will suffice to establish significant risk. There must be a risk that the NCR accused will commit a serious criminal offence."[135]

***Hammoud, Re*, 2018 ONCA 317**—There was no doubt that the appellant suffered from and continues to suffer from a serious mental disorder (schizo-affective disorder) for the past thirty years and there is no doubt that the appellant would discontinue her medication if given the opportunity. These are not the risks at which the "significant threat" threshold is directed. The Board did not conduct the required analysis either of the risk of psychological harm or of the potential gravity of that risk. When read as a whole, the Board's reasons reveal the legal error that the Board failed to apply the proper test for "significant threat to the safety of the public" to the evidence.[136]

***Marchese, Re*, 2018 ONCA 307**—Although the Board's finding that the accused remained a significant threat to the public's safety was reasonable based on the evidence, the Board failed to provide meaningful reasons for rejecting a conditional discharge. The Board's order was not interfered with, but the court set out that the brevity of the Board's treatment of the key issue of significant threat to the safety of the public—only one paragraph at the end of five pages of reasons—was cause for concern and led the Board to treat material evidence without the rigour expected from such a specialized tribunal.[137]

Note: In both ***Hammoud, Re*, 2018 ONCA 317** and ***Marchese, Re*, 2018 ONCA 307**, the court found that the Board's reasons for its dispositions were deficient.

***McAnuff, Re*, [2024] O.J. No. 1806 (C.A.)** — The fact that the accused has not been violent since the index offence does not necessarily establish that they are not a significant threat to the safety of the public. Where the accused lacks insight into his illness and persists with cannabis use that gives him "special powers" and causes him to be irritable and angry and would, if discharged discontinue his medications and resume cannabis use, the Board may properly find that the accused constitutes a significant threat to the safety of the public.

In *McAnuff*, the Board noted that the accused's insight into his mental condition, its symptomatology, the role of treatment, effects of substance use, and risk of re-offence remained limited. The accused did not believe that he suffered from a mental disorder, nor was he able to appreciate the manifestations of psychosis. He did not believe that he required psychiatric treatment and was motivated to take medications due to external reasons. He did not appreciate the fact that his mental condition deteriorated when using substances. Though the accused had not been physically violent since the index offences (assaults), decompensation and irritability continued to occur when using cannabis to the point where he becomes delusional and agitated, requiring chemical restraint. If released into the community, the accused would immediately commence using marijuana. The Court of Appeal will only interfere with the Board's findings where its decision is unreasonable or if the Board made an error of law. The Board's finding that the accused remains a significant threat to the safety of the public was reasonable on the basis of the evidence adduced.

---

134 *Re Medcof*, 2018 ONCA 299 at paras. 55–57 [*Medcof*].

135 *Ibid.* at para. 26.

136 *Hammoud, Re*, 2018 ONCA 317 at paras. 8–9.

137 *Marchese, Re*, 2018 ONCA 307 at para. 10.

APPLICATION—CONSIDERATION OF THE EVIDENCE

***Muthulingam, Re*, 2020 ONCA 680**—Although it is "ill-advised and unnecessary"[138] to copy the Review Board's reasons from the previous year, a new hearing is not warranted where the finding that the significant threat threshold was met was reasonable and supported by evidence adduced at the hearing.

***Murray, Re*, 2020 ONCA 547**—Notwithstanding "positive features" (including the accused's intelligence, his more remote history of being gainfully employed and making a meaningful contribution to society, his lack of aggression toward staff during detention, and his compliance with unit rules), the Board is entitled to find that the accused posed a serious threat. In this case, the accused had a history of improvising and carrying weapons, admitted that he was prepared to use weapons to protect himself from perceived threats, and escaped from hospital staff for six days during an escorted pass.[139]

***Yunus-Ali, Re*, 2020 ONCA 669**—An NCR accused's lack of insight into their mental illness is not a ground for detention in itself, but a lack of insight is a relevant consideration when linked to a risk of harm to the public. The accused's lack of insight related to his need for medication and the impact of substance use.[140] The Board found that "the appellant's lack of insight into his mental illness, the relationship between his mental illness and his propensity for violence against others, his need for medication to control his mental illness, and the risk that substance use would provoke psychosis and risk of violence all created risk of physical harm to the public."[141]

***Sim, Re*, 2019 ONCA 719**—The Board's disposition was unreasonable because it failed to conduct a proper assessment of whether the accused posed a significant threat to the safety of the public. The Board's analysis was improperly dominated by consideration of whether the accused possessed sufficient insight into the effect of cannabis use on his mental condition.[142] Lack of insight into one's mental illness is not a ground for detention in itself.[143] The insight of the NCR accused must be assessed in the context of the entirety of the record before the Board.[144]

***Woods, Re*, 2019 ONCA 87**—Lack of insight has its place in the overall clinical picture, but it must not dominate the significant threat analysis. This consideration alone cannot form the basis for indeterminate detention under Part XX.1 of the *Criminal Code*.[145] In this case, the Board's decision was reasonable, and no legal errors were committed by the Board in reaching its decision.

***Sokal, Re*, 2018 ONCA 113**—The NCR accused's appeal from an order continuing his conditional discharge was allowed. The NCR accused had been living in the community independently since 2014 on conditions that included abstaining from drugs and alcohol. The accused used drugs twice in the eighteen months prior to the disposition.[146] The Board erred in concluding that the NCR accused posed a significant risk because of these two incidents of drug use given evidence of the NCR accused's medication compliance, lack of violence and aggression, ten-month drug-free

138 *Muthulingam, Re*, 2020 ONCA 680 at para. 28.

139 *Murray, Re*, 2020 ONCA 547 at paras. 11–13.

140 *Yunus-Ali, Re*, 2020 ONCA 669 at para. 6.

141 *Ibid.* at para. 9.

142 *Sim, Re*, 2019 ONCA 719 at paras. 16–17.

143 *Ibid.* at para. 22, citing *Kalra, Re*, 2018 ONCA 833 at para. 52.

144 *Ibid.* at para. 21.

145 *Woods, Re*, 2019 ONCA 87 at para. 17.

146 *Sokal, Re*, 2018 ONCA 113 at para. 24.

period, admission to the Hamilton Program for Schizophrenia, and a lack of psychotic symptoms associated with recent drug use.[147]

***Haye, Re*, 2011 ONCA 700**—On the issue of assessing whether an NCRMD accused remains a significant threat to the safety of the public, it is a reversible error for the Review Board to misstate the evidence of a psychiatrist and to fail to refer to other relevant evidence.

***Chang, Re*, [2024] O.J. No. 1441 (C.A.)** — Where there is a joint submission for a particular disposition that includes "detention, subject to conditions with community living privileges" the Board errs where it fails to consider a less restrictive disposition.

EXPERT EVIDENCE PERMITTED

***Re Medcof*, 2018 ONCA 299**—It is not unreasonable for the Board to rely on the NCR accused's history of violence as part of its assessment of the expert evidence:[148] "While the conduct must be criminal in nature, not all criminal conduct will suffice to establish significant risk. There must be a risk that the NCR accused will commit a serious criminal offence."[149]

***Pellett, Re*, 2017 ONCA 753** —Evidence of non-compliance with medication should not be improperly extrapolated by the Board to support its conclusion that the appellant poses a significant threat to the safety of the public when there is otherwise insufficient evidence to support that finding. Whether the appellant would act out in a way contemplated by section 672.54 was purely speculative. In this case, the index offence appeared to be a "one-off incident."[150]

***Coburn, Re*, 2016 ONCA 536**—A conditional discharge is not suitable where the NCR accused is incapable of providing consent to treatment, as was the case here. Appeal dismissed from the Ontario Review Board's decision that the NCR accused remained a significant risk to the public, necessitating the continuation of the detention order on the same terms and conditions. Expert psychiatric evidence "demonstrated the likelihood of Ms. Coburn's re-engaging in the criminal harassment of strangers provided an adequate basis for the conclusion that the threshold test had been met."[151] At para. 19: "A critical distinction between a conditional discharge and a detention order lies in the means by which an NCR accused can be involuntarily returned to the hospital." Immediate intervention to address the accused's threatening behaviour would be helpful; this could not be achieved by the *Mental Health Act* alone, so a conditional discharge was not sufficient to respond to the risk posed by the accused.

***Schutzman, Re*, 2013 ONCA 48** —The ORB has repeatedly accepted that reliance on expert medical evidence is a valid basis for finding that an NCR accused remains a significant threat to the safety of the public. This is one example. From para. 5, the ORB at the hearing that the appellant remained a significant threat to the safety of the public. This was based on overwhelming expert opinion evidence (as well as the appellant's own evidence) that the appellant would immediately stop all medication if he were unsupervised. The Board found that without medication the appellant's condition would deteriorate, he would become delusional and would then engage in threatening behaviour that would result in a significant risk of harm to the public.

---

147 *Ibid.* at paras. 25–26.
148 *Medcof*, above note 132 at paras. 55–57.
149 *Ibid.* at para. 26.
150 *Pellett, Re*, 2017 ONCA 753 at para. 30.
151 *Coburn, Re*, 2016 ONCA 536 at para. 17.

REJECTING EXPERT EVIDENCE

***Laberakis, Re*, 2012 ONCA 70**—Where the Board rejects expert evidence, it must base its decision on the evidence. The Review Board is not required to follow the opinions of the expert or the hospital, but the Board's decision must be based on evidence. The appropriate threshold of risk must be applied when considering the issue of whether the accused remains a significant threat to the safety of the public. In this case, the Board's concerns about the accused's insight and that it could not be said the accused would seek help if needed, placed an inappropriate burden on the accused.

For contrast, see also ***Le Feuvre, Re*, 2012 ONCA 843**. Although the Board did not agree with the expert's recommendation in this case, the expert's evidence was a "more than sufficient basis" (para. 2) to conclude their order represented the least onerous, least restrictive disposition at the time.

* * * * *

Victim impact statement

672.541 If a verdict of not criminally responsible on account of mental disorder has been rendered in respect of an accused, the court or Review Board shall

(a) at a hearing held under section 672.45, 672.47, 672.64, 672.81 or 672.82 or subsection 672.84(5), take into consideration any statement filed by a victim in accordance with subsection 672.5(14) in determining the appropriate disposition or conditions under section 672.54, to the extent that the statement is relevant to its consideration of the criteria set out in section 672.54;

(b) at a hearing held under section 672.64 or subsection 672.84(3), take into consideration any statement filed by a victim in accordance with subsection 672.5(14), to the extent that the statement is relevant to its consideration of the criteria set out in subsection 672.64(1) or 672.84(3), as the case may be, in deciding whether to find that the accused is a high-risk accused, or to revoke such a finding; and

(c) at a hearing held under section 672.81 or 672.82 in respect of a high-risk accused, take into consideration any statement filed by a victim in accordance with subsection 672.5(14) in determining whether to refer to the court for review the finding that the accused is a high-risk accused, to the extent that the statement is relevant to its consideration of the criteria set out in subsection 672.84(1).

1999, c. 25, s. 12 (Preamble); 2005, c. 22, s. 21; 2014, c. 6, s. 10

Additional conditions—safety and security

672.542 When a court or Review Board holds a hearing referred to in section 672.5, the court or Review Board shall consider whether it is desirable, in the interests of the safety and security of any person, particularly a victim of or witness to the offence or a justice system participant, to include as a condition of the disposition that the accused

(a) abstain from communicating, directly or indirectly, with any victim, witness or other person identified in the disposition, or refrain from going to any place specified in the disposition; or

(b) comply with any other condition specified in the disposition that the court or Review Board considers necessary to ensure the safety and security of those persons.

2014, c. 6, s. 10

Treatment not a condition

672.55 (1) No disposition made under section 672.54 shall direct that any psychiatric or other treatment of the accused be carried out or that the accused submit to such treatment except that the disposition may include a condition regarding psychiatric or other treatment where the accused has consented to the condition and the court or Review Board considers the condition to be reasonable and necessary in the interests of the accused.

(2) [Repealed, 2005, c. 22, s. 22]

1991, c. 43, s. 4; 1997, c. 18, s. 86; 2005, c. 22, s. 22

CASELAW

***Ohenhen, Re*, 2018 ONCA 65**—An accused found not criminally responsible on account of mental disorder and incapable of consenting to their own treatment under the *Health Care Consent Act* is capable of fulfilling the section 672.55(1) consent requirement (i.e., the consent necessary for a disposition under section 672.54 to direct psychiatric or other treatment). The capacity required to consent to a condition under section 672.55(1) is the ability to understand all information relevant to the operation of the condition and to appreciate all reasonably foreseeable consequences of agreeing to the condition.[152]

*****

Delegated authority to vary restrictions on liberty of accused

672.56 (1) A Review Board that makes a disposition in respect of an accused under paragraph 672.54(b) or (c) may delegate to the person in charge of the hospital authority to direct that the restrictions on the liberty of the accused be increased or decreased within any limits and subject to any conditions set out in that disposition, and any direction so made is deemed for the purposes of this Act to be a disposition made by the Review Board.

Exception—high-risk accused

(1.1) If the accused is a high-risk accused, any direction is subject to the restrictions set out in subsection 672.64(3).

Notice to accused and Review Board of increase in restrictions

(2) A person who increases the restrictions on the liberty of the accused significantly pursuant to authority delegated to the person by a Review Board shall

(a) make a record of the increased restrictions on the file of the accused; and

(b) give notice of the increase as soon as is practicable to the accused and, if the increased restrictions remain in force for a period exceeding seven days, to the Review Board.

1991, c. 43, s. 4; 2014, c. 6, s. 11

CASELAW

RESTRICTION HEARINGS

***Tran, Re*, 2020 ONCA 722**—The NCR accused's mental state and behaviour changed, including possible mental deterioration, and as a result his indirectly supervised off-unit privileges were placed on hold. The accused sought a review hearing with respect to the alleged increased restriction of his liberty. The Review Board determined that a notice of restriction of liberty was not required and that the appropriate disposition was continued detention, with specified privileges and conditions. The Board did not err in continuing detention; a conditional discharge was not appropriate given the accused's record, his significant risk to public safety, and the seriousness

152 Content reproduced in part with permission from *Fitness to Stand Trial*, above note 12 at Appendix A, 200.

of the index offences.[153] The significance inquiry must be informed by the discretion afforded to the hospital to engage in day-to-day management decisions.[154] Although the Board erred in conflating the two parts of the *Campbell* test, the Board did not err in determining that the increase in restrictions was not significant. The court declined to endorse the Attorney General's proposed procedures on notices and hearings under sections 672.56(2) and 672.81(2.1). It is not the role of the Court of Appeal to dictate the Board's approach on this issue. Providing a directive to that end could impinge on the "Board's jurisdiction to fashion its own rules of procedure and practice and the exercise of its discretion."[155]

***Campbell, Re*, 2018 ONCA 140**—First, a finding must be made as to whether there is in fact an increase in restrictions, giving consideration to the accused's liberty status before and after; only after an increase has been established, the second part of the analysis considers whether the increase is "significant," thereby triggering notice and a mandatory hearing. A contextual, individualized approach from the perspective of "a reasonable person, considering all of the circumstances"[156] should be adopted in this second part of the test. At para. 64, "the purpose of s. 672.56(2) is to act as a final liberty safeguard allowing for a second-look at those hospital decisions that have such serious ramifications for the liberty of the NCR accused, that they should be examined ahead of the next yearly review."[157] A case-by-case approach and individualized assessment are to be adopted with respect to the notice requirement under section 672.56(2).[158] In section 672.81(2.1), the meaning of "significantly increase" attracts a standard of correctness as it engages a question of law while the reasonableness standard applies to the Board's application of the *Campbell* test.[159]

***R. v. Petroniuk*, 2014 ONSC 6951**—Section 672.56(2) of the *Criminal Code* does not violate section 7 of the *Charter*. The procedure in the provision is a fair one, such a review is discretionary, and the principles of fundamental justice do not entitle a *Charter* applicant to a particular type of process or ideal procedure.

Note: See also **section 672.81(2.1)** and ***Saikaley***, below.

***Saikaley, Re*, 2012 ONCA 92**—There is no evidence to conclude that "as soon as practicable" under section 672.81(2.1) means that a restriction hearing should be held within thirty days from the date notice is received. Hearings and decisions to which patients are entitled should be rendered "as expeditiously as is practicable."[160] Parliament did not impose a set time frame and instead used the flexible language of "as soon as practicable." Parliament clearly intended that restriction hearings should be set, held, and concluded expeditiously. Where a patient's liberty has been significantly restricted, an expeditious hearing provides an important safeguard.[161]

***C. (M.L.) v. Ontario (Review Board)*, 2010 ONCA 843**—The standard of correctness applies to determinations of law.[162] The Review Board's review of increased restrictions imposed by the hospital on an NCR accused's liberty is not limited to a patient's circumstances at the time of

153 Index offences in this case: attempted murder, assault with a weapon, and endangering life while committing assault.
154 *Tran, Re*, 2020 ONCA 722 at paras. 63–64.
155 *Ibid.* at para. 78.
156 *Ibid.* at para. 67.
157 *Ibid.* at para. 64.
158 *Ibid.* at para. 68.
159 *Ibid.* at para. 28.
160 *Saikaley, Re*, 2012 ONCA 92 at para. 72.
161 *Ibid.* at para. 68.
162 *C. (M.L.) v. Ontario (Review Board)*, 2010 ONCA 843 at para. 21.

the restriction decision. The Board is mandated to consider the indefinite nature of the hospital's decision and the ongoing circumstances of the NCR accused from the time of the restriction decision up to and including the time of the review.[163] The applicable standard on a restrictions review is whether the decision to restrict the patient's liberty met the "least onerous and least restrictive" test as set out in section 672.54.[164]

* * * * *

Warrant of committal

672.57 Where the court or Review Board makes a disposition under paragraph 672.54(c), it shall issue a warrant of committal of the accused, which may be in Form 49.

1991, c. 43, s. 4

Treatment disposition

672.58 Where a verdict of unfit to stand trial is rendered and the court has not made a disposition under section 672.54 in respect of an accused, the court may, on application by the prosecutor, by order, direct that treatment of the accused be carried out for a specified period not exceeding sixty days, subject to such conditions as the court considers appropriate and, where the accused is not detained in custody, direct that the accused submit to that treatment by the person or at the hospital specified.

1991, c. 43, s. 4

CASELAW

HOSPITAL CONSENT

***R. v. Conception*, 2014 SCC 60**—The hospital's consent is required in relation to all aspects of a disposition order made under section 672.58. Without that consent, the court cannot make the order. The requirement of consent in section 672.58 is not procedurally unfair and is not unconstitutionally vague or arbitrary. Although it would be exceedingly rare, the S.C.C. did not rule out the possibility that in other cases, a potential violation of section 7 *Charter* rights could result from the hospital withholding consent in a particular case.[165]

* * * * *

Criteria for disposition

672.59 (1) No disposition may be made under section 672.58 unless the court is satisfied, on the basis of the testimony of a medical practitioner, that a specific treatment should be administered to the accused for the purpose of making the accused fit to stand trial.

Evidence required

(2) The testimony required by the court for the purposes of subsection (1) shall include a statement that the medical practitioner has made an assessment of the accused and is of the opinion, based on the grounds specified, that

(a) the accused, at the time of the assessment, was unfit to stand trial;

(b) the psychiatric treatment and any other related medical treatment specified by the medical practitioner will likely make the accused fit to stand trial within a period not exceeding sixty days and that without that treatment the accused is likely to remain unfit to stand trial;

163 *Ibid.* at para. 39.

164 *Ibid.* at paras. 43–44.

165 Note that while consent is a prerequisite, the court will have the ultimate discretion in urgent situations.

(c) the risk of harm to the accused from the psychiatric and other related medical treatment specified is not disproportionate to the benefit anticipated to be derived from it; and
(d) the psychiatric and other related medical treatment specified is the least restrictive and least intrusive treatment that could, in the circumstances, be specified for the purpose referred to in subsection (1), considering the opinions referred to in paragraphs (b) and (c).

1991, c. 43, s. 4

Notice required

672.6 (1) The court shall not make a disposition under section 672.58 unless the prosecutor notifies the accused, in writing and as soon as practicable, of the application.

Challenge by accused

(2) On receiving the notice referred to in subsection (1), the accused may challenge the application and adduce evidence for that purpose.

1991, c. 43, s. 4; 1997, c. 18, s. 87

Exception

672.61 (1) The court shall not direct, and no disposition made under section 672.58 shall include, the performance of psychosurgery or electro-convulsive therapy or any other prohibited treatment that is prescribed.

Definitions

(2) In this section,

electro-convulsive therapy means a procedure for the treatment of certain mental disorders that induces, by electrical stimulation of the brain, a series of generalized convulsions; (*sismothérapie*)

psychosurgery means any procedure that by direct or indirect access to the brain removes, destroys or interrupts the continuity of histologically normal brain tissue, or inserts indwelling electrodes for pulsed electrical stimulation for the purpose of altering behaviour or treating psychiatric illness, but does not include neurological procedures used to diagnose or treat intractable physical pain, organic brain conditions, or epilepsy, where any of those conditions is clearly demonstrable. (*psychochirurgie*)

1991, c. 43, s. 4

Consent of hospital required for treatment

672.62 (1) No court shall make a disposition under section 672.58 without the consent of
(a) the person in charge of the hospital where the accused is to be treated; or
(b) the person to whom responsibility for the treatment of the accused is assigned by the court.

CASELAW

***Centre for Addiction and Mental Health v. Al-Sherewadi*, 2011 ONSC 2272**—There is nothing in the wording of section 672.62(1) that imposes a time limit on the consent of the hospital or that requires that the consent be immediate and unqualified.

* * * * *

Consent of accused not required for treatment

(2) The court may direct that treatment of an accused be carried out pursuant to a disposition made under section 672.58 without the consent of the accused or a person who, according to the laws of the province where the disposition is made, is authorized to consent for the accused.

1991, c. 43, s. 4

Effective date of disposition

672.63 A disposition shall come into force on the day on which it is made or on any later day that the court or Review Board specifies in it, and shall remain in force until the Review Board holds a hearing to review the disposition and makes another disposition.

1991, c. 43, s. 4; 2005, c. 22, s. 23

CASELAW

***Kazi, Re*, 2025 ONCA 375** —When a new disposition is issued, the previous disposition no longer governs or applies to the appellant.[166]

Halat, *Re*, 2019 ONCA 112 —This case provides a helpful summary of the law governing whether a case or appeal is moot. At paras. 7 to 10:

> [7] The seminal case from the Supreme Court of Canada on the question of when a court should exercise its discretion to hear a moot case or appeal is *Borowski v. Canada (Attorney General)*, [1989] 1 S.C.R. 342 (S.C.C.), where the court mandated a two-step process for the analysis. **The first step is to decide whether the case or appeal is moot, i.e. whether there remains a live controversy that affects the rights of the parties. If there is not and the case or appeal is therefore moot, the general rule is that the court will not hear the matter.**
>
> [8] However, **the court must decide whether it should exercise its discretion to hear and decide the case or appeal in any event, considering three factors:** 1) whether the necessary **adversarial context** remains, which may be provided by collateral consequences of the resolution of the issue between the parties; 2) despite the concern for judicial economy, whether **special circumstances** justify applying scarce judicial resources to the case because, for example, the case raises an important issue that will always be moot by the time it reaches appeal, or an issue that is a matter of public importance and in the public interest to resolve; 3) the need for the court to be aware of its proper **law-making function** and the extent to which it may be departing from its traditional role by hearing the case or appeal: *Borowski*, at pp. 358-63.
>
> [9] In answer to the first stage of the two-step analysis, it is clear that the appeal is moot because the 2018 disposition of the Board no longer governs or applies to the appellant. It is spent and of no further effect. There is therefore no live issue between the parties in relation to that disposition.
>
> [10] The second step is whether the court should hear the moot appeal in any event [Emphasis added].

High-Risk Accused

Finding

672.64 (1) On application made by the prosecutor before any disposition to discharge an accused absolutely, the court may, at the conclusion of a hearing, find the accused to be a high-risk accused if the accused has been found not criminally responsible on account of mental disorder for a serious personal injury offence, as defined in subsection 672.81(1.3), the accused was 18 years of age or more at the time of the commission of the offence and

(a) the court is satisfied that there is a substantial likelihood that the accused will use violence that could endanger the life or safety of another person; or

---

166 *Kazi, Re*, 2025 ONCA 375 at para. 23.

(b) the court is of the opinion that the acts that constitute the offence were of such a brutal nature as to indicate a risk of grave physical or psychological harm to another person.

Factors to consider

(2) In deciding whether to find that the accused is a high-risk accused, the court shall consider all relevant evidence, including

(a) the nature and circumstances of the offence;

(b) any pattern of repetitive behaviour of which the offence forms a part;

(c) the accused's current mental condition;

(d) the past and expected course of the accused's treatment, including the accused's willingness to follow treatment; and

(e) the opinions of experts who have examined the accused.

Detention of high-risk accused

(3) If the court finds the accused to be a high-risk accused, the court shall make a disposition under paragraph 672.54(c), but the accused's detention must not be subject to any condition that would permit the accused to be absent from the hospital unless

(a) it is appropriate, in the opinion of the person in charge of the hospital, for the accused to be absent from the hospital for medical reasons or for any purpose that is necessary for the accused's treatment, if the accused is escorted by a person who is authorized by the person in charge of the hospital; and

(b) a structured plan has been prepared to address any risk related to the accused's absence and, as a result, that absence will not present an undue risk to the public.

Appeal

(4) A decision not to find an accused to be a high-risk accused is deemed to be a disposition for the purpose of sections 672.72 to 672.78.

For greater certainty

(5) For greater certainty, a finding that an accused is a high-risk accused is a disposition and sections 672.72 to 672.78 apply to it.

1991, c. 43, s. 4; 2005, c. 22, s. 24; 2014, c. 6, s. 12

672.65 and 672.66 [No sections 672.65 and 672.66]

CASELAW

***R. v. Schoenborn*, [2015] B.C.J. No. 2619**—The high-risk offender provisions apply retrospectively to acts committed before the provisions came into force.

***R. v. Schoenborn* (2017), 354 C.C.C. (3d) 393 (B.C.S.C.)**—"Substantial likelihood" of violence as provided in section **672.64(1)(a)** means a degree of risk greater than that of "significant threat."

FACTORS TO CONSIDER

***R v. Hadfield*, 2024 ONCA 46** — In deciding whether to find that the accused is a high-risk accused, the court shall consider all relevant evidence, including:

(a) the nature and circumstances of the offence;

(b) any pattern of repetitive behaviour of which the offence forms a part;

(c) the accused's current mental condition;

(d) the past and expected course of the accused's treatment, including the accused's willingness to follow treatment; and
(e) the opinions of experts who have examined the accused.[167]

The above factors are not prerequisites nor an exhaustive list. The court's imposition of an HRA designation will be found to be reasonable where the court is satisfied to a high degree of probability on all of the evidence that unrestrained and untreated, the accused will use violence that could endanger the life or safety of another person.

***R. v. Teggart*, 2025 ONCA 431 – The Court found that the criteria is met where the accused:**

1) continued to suffer from delusions, in particular that family members were imposters;
2) harboured anger toward family members;
3) had a mental disorder that was treatment resistant; and
4) had symptoms that were escalating over the previous few years.

* * * * *

Dual Status Offenders

Where court imposes a sentence

672.67 (1) Where a court imposes a sentence of imprisonment on an offender who is, or thereby becomes, a dual status offender, that sentence takes precedence over any prior custodial disposition, pending any placement decision by the Review Board.

Custodial disposition by court

(2) Where a court imposes a custodial disposition on an accused who is, or thereby becomes, a dual status offender, the disposition takes precedence over any prior sentence of imprisonment pending any placement decision by the Review Board.

1991, c. 43, s. 4; 1995, c. 22, s. 10; 2005, c. 22, s. 25

Definition of Minister

672.68 (1) In this section and in sections 672.69 and 672.7, Minister means the Minister of Public Safety and Emergency Preparedness or the Minister responsible for correctional services of the province to which a dual status offender may be sent pursuant to a sentence of imprisonment.

Placement decision by Review Board

(2) On application by the Minister or of its own motion, where the Review Board is of the opinion that the place of custody of a dual status offender pursuant to a sentence or custodial disposition made by the court is inappropriate to meet the mental health needs of the offender or to safeguard the well-being of other persons, the Review Board shall, after giving the offender and the Minister reasonable notice, decide whether to place the offender in custody in a hospital or in a prison.

CASELAW

***Walker v. Ontario (Attorney General)*, 2019 ONCA 957, application for leave dismissed [2020] S.C.C.A. No. 136**—The Board advised the dual status offender that if a significant change in the offender's circumstances was evident at the review hearing, then the Board would likely order a placement hearing for a subsequent date as required in that circumstance by section 672.69(2) of the *Criminal Code*. Walker would be requesting a transfer from a penitentiary to a mental health

167 *R. v. Hadfield*, 2024 ONCA 46 at para. 14.

care centre at a placement hearing, if scheduled. The Board found that there was insufficient evidence to establish a change in circumstances and, as a result, was not obligated to schedule a placement hearing. The dual status offender's therapeutic needs were met in the penitentiary and the mental health care centre did not treat sexual offenders, which the accused was. The Court of Appeal dismissed the appeal. The Board did not err in deciding not to schedule a placement hearing. At para. 22: "On the Review Board's interpretation of the *Code*, a significant change in the circumstances of the offender is a prerequisite to the Review Board granting a request to schedule a placement hearing on the offender's application. The Review Board is interpreting its home statute and its interpretation is entitled to deference."

***Waypoint Centre for Mental Health Care v. R.*, 2014 ONCA 182** — At para. 24, the court set out the following:

> [T]he test for suspending a placement decision pending appeal should be substantially the same as the test for suspending a disposition pending appeal. I rely on two considerations. First, the *Code* prescribes that, in either case, the focus must be on the mental condition of the accused. Second, in either case, the Board's assessment of an accused's mental condition is entitled to significant deference from this court. This assessment lies within the Board's specialized expertise on matters of psychiatry and mental health. If its assessment is reasonable, this court will not interfere.

*****

Idem

(3) In making a placement decision, the Review Board shall take into consideration

(a) the need to protect the public from dangerous persons;

(b) the treatment needs of the offender and the availability of suitable treatment resources to address those needs;

(c) whether the offender would consent to or is a suitable candidate for treatment;

(d) any submissions made to the Review Board by the offender or any other party to the proceedings and any assessment report submitted in writing to the Review Board; and

(e) any other factors that the Review Board considers relevant.

Time for making placement decision

(4) The Review Board shall make its placement decision as soon as practicable but not later than thirty days after receiving an application from, or giving notice to, the Minister under subsection (2), unless the Review Board and the Minister agree to a longer period not exceeding sixty days.

Effects of placement decision

(5) Where the offender is detained in a prison pursuant to the placement decision of the Review Board, the Minister is responsible for the supervision and control of the offender.

1991, c. 43, s. 4; 2005, c. 10, s. 34

Minister and Review Board entitled to access

672.69 (1) The Minister and the Review Board are entitled to have access to any dual status offender in respect of whom a placement decision has been made, for the purpose of conducting a review of the sentence or disposition imposed.

Review of placement decisions

(2) The Review Board shall hold a hearing as soon as is practicable to review a placement decision, on application by the Minister or the dual status offender who is the subject of the decision, where the Review Board is satisfied that a significant change in circumstances requires it.

Idem

(3) The Review Board may of its own motion hold a hearing to review a placement decision after giving the Minister and the dual status offender who is subject to it reasonable notice.

Minister shall be a party

(4) The Minister shall be a party in any proceedings relating to the placement of a dual status offender.

1991, c. 43, s. 4; 2005, c. 22, s. 42(F)

Notice of discharge

672.7 (1) Where the Minister or the Review Board intends to discharge a dual status offender from custody, each shall give written notice to the other indicating the time, place and conditions of the discharge.

Warrant of committal

(2) A Review Board that makes a placement decision shall issue a warrant of committal of the accused, which may be in Form 50.

1991, c. 43, s. 4

Detention to count as service of term

672.71 (1) Each day of detention of a dual status offender pursuant to a placement decision or a custodial disposition shall be treated as a day of service of the term of imprisonment, and the accused shall be deemed, for all purposes, to be lawfully confined in a prison.

Disposition takes precedence over probation orders

(2) When a dual status offender is convicted or discharged on the conditions set out in a probation order made under section 730 in respect of an offence but is not sentenced to a term of imprisonment, the custodial disposition in respect of the accused comes into force and, notwithstanding subsection 732.2(1), takes precedence over any probation order made in respect of the offence.

1991, c. 43, s. 4; 1995, c. 22, s. 10

Appeals

Grounds for appeal

672.72 (1) Any party may appeal against a disposition made by a court or a Review Board, or a placement decision made by a Review Board, to the court of appeal of the province where the disposition or placement decision was made on any ground of appeal that raises a question of law or fact alone or of mixed law and fact.

CASELAW

THE JURISDICTION OF THE COURT OF APPEAL TO SET ASIDE A VERDICT OF NCR

***R. v. Fraser*, [1997] O.J. No. 1282 (C.A.)**—This court's jurisdiction to set aside a finding of not criminally responsible on account of mental disorder on the basis that the finding was unreasonable is the same as this court's power to set aside a conviction for that reason. The appellant must demonstrate that a trier of fact acting reasonably and properly applying the law could not have arrived at the finding of not criminally responsible on account of mental disorder. If the evidence provided a reasonable basis for a finding, on the balance of probabilities, that the appellant operated under either of the incapacities described in section 16(1) of the *Criminal Code* then this ground of appeal must fail.[168]

***R v. Clyke*, [2024] N.S.J. No. 335 (C.A.)** — In exceptional circumstances, the Court of Appeal may reopen a previously decided appeal where the appeal had not been dismissed on the merits. In *Clyke,* the accused had abandoned his appeal to have his conviction overturned on the basis that he was not criminally responsible at the time of the offence. In deciding to reopen the appeal, the Nova Scotia Court of Appeal relied upon the decision of the Ontario Court of Appeal in *R. v. Scott,*[169] in particular, at para. 33:

> Under any formulation, jurisdiction to reopen after a formal order has been issued is precluded where there has been a hearing at which merit-based arguments were made and a decision that is based on the panel's appreciation of the merits of the appeal, as opposed to a basis independent of the merits. For example, an appeal that was heard on the merits but was then dismissed because the appellant abandoned it would not fall into the *Rhingo* formulation or any of the later formulations of when jurisdiction is precluded.

The court noted that the accused had abandoned his appeal when he was emotionally upset and without the benefit of counsel.

APPLICATION — REVIEW BOARD AS INTERVENOR ON APPEAL

***McGinty v. Yukon (Director of Mental Wellness and Substance Use Services)*, 2024 YKCA 10** — On appeal from the continued detention order made by the Yukon Review Board ("YRB"), the Court granted the YRB's application under the public interest basis for intervenor status. The appellant was an Indigenous person who had been found NCR and detained in a forensic psychiatric hospital. The Court of Appeal found that the Board "is uniquely positioned to offer its specialized expertise on the application of Gladue principles within the regional context of the Yukon ... These insights are particularly valuable in light of the broader impact the Court's ruling may have on similarly situated review boards across the country."[170]

APPLICATION — CASE EXAMPLES OF APPEAL TO BOARD'S DISPOSITION

***Murray, Re*, 2017 ONCA 731** — This case is an example of a dismissed appeal of a Board's disposition ordering detention. In the initial disposition, the Board ordered the accused's detention to a general forensic unit of a hospital. The Board subsequently ordered the accused detained on a secure forensic unit of the hospital, with the same privileges as contained in the initial disposition. The Board's decision to continue detention in a secure forensic unit was reasonable and the finding that the accused continued to pose a significant threat to the safety of the public was supported by the evidence: the accused lacked insight into his major mental illness and need for medication; had prior convictions for assault, uttering threats, and assault with a weapon; and the treatment team held the unanimous opinion that the accused met the threshold for being a significant threat to the safety of the public.

***Krueger v. Ontario (Criminal Code Review Board)* (1994), 95 C.C.C. (3d) 88 (Ont. C.A.)** —There is no appeal with respect to the Board's declining a recommendation to transfer the accused to another province.

---

168 *R. v. Fraser*, [1997] O.J. No. 1282 at para. 19 (C.A.).

169 *R. v. Scott*, 2023 ONCA 820.

170 *McGinty v. Yukon (Director of Mental Wellness and Substance Use Services)*, 2024 YKCA 10 at para. 48.

***Re Chaudry* (2015), 324 C.C.C. (3d) 281 (Ont. C.A.)**—The Court of Appeal has jurisdiction to review the Board's decision regarding a restriction of liberty hearing.

* * * * *

Limitation period for appeal
(2) An appellant shall give notice of an appeal against a disposition or placement decision in the manner directed by the applicable rules of court within fifteen days after the day on which the appellant receives a copy of the placement decision or disposition and the reasons for it or within any further time that the court of appeal, or a judge of that court, may direct.

Appeal to be heard expeditiously
(3) The court of appeal shall hear an appeal against a disposition or placement decision in or out of the regular sessions of the court, as soon as practicable after the day on which the notice of appeal is given, within any period that may be fixed by the court of appeal, a judge of the court of appeal, or the rules of that court.
1991, c. 43, s. 4; 1997, c. 18, s. 88

Appeal on the transcript
672.73 (1) An appeal against a disposition by a court or Review Board or placement decision by a Review Board shall be based on a transcript of the proceedings and any other evidence that the court of appeal finds necessary to admit in the interests of justice.

Additional evidence
(2) For the purpose of admitting additional evidence under this section, subsections 683(1) and (2) apply, with such modifications as the circumstances require.
1991, c. 43, s. 4

CASELAW

THE TEST ON APPEAL FOR ADMITTING FRESH EVIDENCE

***R. v. Warsing*, [1998] 3 S.C.R. 579**—NCRMD evidence was being led for the first time on appeal in this case. The test for admitting fresh evidence on appeal established by ***R. v. Palmer*, [1980] 1 S.C.R. 759** applied:

> (1) The evidence should generally not be admitted if, by due diligence, it could have been adduced at trial provided that this general principle will not be applied as strictly in a criminal case as in civil cases [citation omitted].
> (2) The evidence must be relevant in the sense that it bears upon a decisive or potentially decisive issue in the trial.
> (3) The evidence must be credible in the sense that it is reasonably capable of belief; and
> (4) It must be such that if believed it could reasonably, when taken with the other evidence adduced at trial, be expected to have affected the result.[171]

APPLICATION—FRESH EVIDENCE IN GENERAL

***R. v. Owen*, 2003 SCC 33**—An absolute discharge with respect to an NCR accused should only be granted after considering all of the reliable evidence available at the time of the Board hearing and, if appealed, at the time of appellate review. In general, it is desirable for an appellate court

171 *R. v. Warsing*, [1998] 3 S.C.R. 579 at para. 50 [citations omitted].

to admit fresh evidence that is trustworthy and touches on the issue of risk to public safety as being necessary in the interests of justice.[172]

***R. v. Wittke*, 2025 ONCA 429** – A motion by the accused for a fresh psychiatric assessment under s. 672.11 was denied on the basis that: (1) the defence's decision not to call the qualified forensic psychiatrist – who, at the *voir dire*, confirmed the diagnoses that the accused now sought to show but could not preclude the accused's ability to form intent for murder – was strategic and not a basis for a further assessment on appeal; and (2) a new assessment was not necessary as it could not reasonably shed light on the accused's psychiatric circumstances eight years earlier, at the time when the offence was committed. There was no evidence that the original report was flawed or that a new assessment would advance an appeal. There was no evidence of any substantive changes since the original **report.**

***Kalra, Re*, 2016 ONCA 390**—If the Board's assessment that maintaining a conditional discharge reflects logical and common-sense reasoning, then its disposition is not unreasonable nor does it reflect a failure of the Board to approach its task in accordance with binding authorities. The Board relied on risk factors including the accused's active symptoms of mental illness, his lack of insight, his refusal to participate in rehabilitative efforts, and his stated intention to stop taking his medication if discharged. The accused's treatment team opined that chances were "very high" the accused would engage in serious criminal misconduct if granted an absolute discharge.[173]

***Centre for Addiction and Mental Health v. R.*, 2014 ONCA 740**—Post-discharge conduct can be relied upon as fresh evidence by a hospital to appeal a Board's disposition. In this case, the fresh evidence met the test for admission under section 672.73(1) and the test for admission of fresh evidence on appeal.

***Furlan, Re*, 2013 ONCA 618**[174]—An application by the Crown for an order suspending an absolute discharge and directing the application of a conditional discharge pending appeal was granted on the basis of fresh evidence that the accused stopped taking his prescribed medication and began drinking and using drugs only weeks after the absolute discharge was granted. The fresh evidence demonstrated that the accused once again represented a threat to public safety due to his mental disorder. The proposed conditional discharge was the least onerous and least restrictive disposition.

***Ontario Shores Centre for Mental Health Sciences v. Darch*, 2010 ONCA 36**—The appeal was allowed and a rehearing by the Board was ordered. The fresh evidence demonstrated that within a short time after being absolutely discharged, the accused acted in a manner contrary to several of the factors relied upon by the Board to ground its decision and in a manner causing his out-patient psychiatrist to view the accused as posing a significant risk to the safety of the public. The fresh evidence undermined several of the Board's reasons in granting an absolute discharge and materially impacted the factual foundation for its disposition. The fresh evidence could reasonably have affected the result of the Board hearing.[175]

---

172 *Owen*, above note 113 at paras. 59 and 71.

173 *Ibid.* at paras. 15–16.

174 This case follows the principles set out in *Conway v. Brockville Psychiatric Hospital* (1994), 18 O.R. (3d) 27 (C.A.) [*Conway*]; *Northeast Mental Health Centre v. Rogers*, 2007 ONCA 561; and *Penetanguishene Mental Health Centre v. Ontario (Attorney General)*, [2001] O.J. No. 1074 (C.A.).

175 *Darch*, above note 112 at paras. 31–32.

APPLICATION — REMEDIES

R. v. M. (I.E.)*, [2003] O.J. No. 953 (C.A.)** — Section 686(1) of the *Criminal Code* gives the Court of Appeal the jurisdiction to quash a conviction and find the appellant NCRMD: "Indeed when the NCRMD defence is raised for the first time on appeal this, rather than a new trial, would appear to be the presumptive course."[176] Citing ***R. v. Warsing[177] at para. 65, the Court of Appeal will in most cases likely have sufficient evidence to determine the NCRMD question and it is only in cases where the facts are complex and further evidence is required that a new trial would be ordered.

* * * * *

Notice of appeal to be given to court or Review Board

672.74 (1) The clerk of the court of appeal, on receiving notice of an appeal against a disposition or placement decision, shall notify the court or Review Board that made the disposition.

Transmission of records to court of appeal

(2) On receipt of notification under subsection (1), the court or Review Board shall transmit to the court of appeal, before the time that the appeal is to be heard or within any time that the court of appeal or a judge of that court may direct,

(a) a copy of the disposition or placement decision;

(b) all exhibits filed with the court or Review Board or a copy of them; and

(c) all other material in its possession respecting the hearing.

Record to be kept by court of appeal

(3) The clerk of the court of appeal shall keep the material referred to in subsection (2) with the records of the court of appeal.

Appellant to provide transcript of evidence

(4) Unless it is contrary to an order of the court of appeal or any applicable rules of court, the appellant shall provide the court of appeal and the respondent with a transcript of any evidence taken before a court or Review Board by a stenographer or a sound recording apparatus, certified by the stenographer or in accordance with subsection 540(6), as the case may be.

Saving

(5) An appeal shall not be dismissed by the court of appeal by reason only that a person other than the appellant failed to comply with this section.

1991, c. 43, s. 4; 2005, c. 22, s. 42(F)

Automatic suspension of certain dispositions

672.75 The filing of a notice of appeal against a disposition made under section 672.58 suspends the application of the disposition pending the determination of the appeal.

1991, c. 43, s. 4; 2014, c. 6, s. 13

Application respecting dispositions under appeal

672.76 (1) Any party who gives notice to each of the other parties, within the time and in the manner prescribed, may apply to a judge of the court of appeal for an order under this section respecting a disposition or placement decision that is under appeal.

---

176 *R. v. M. (I.E.)*, [2003] O.J. No. 953 at para. 46 (C.A.).

177 [1998] 3 S.C.R. 579.

Discretionary powers respecting suspension of dispositions

(2) On receipt of an application made pursuant to subsection (1) a judge of the court of appeal may, if satisfied that the mental condition of the accused justifies it,

(a) by order, direct that a disposition made under section 672.58 be carried out pending the determination of the appeal, despite section 672.75;

(a.1) by order, direct that a disposition made under paragraph 672.54(a) be suspended pending the determination of the appeal;

(b) by order, direct that the application of a placement decision or a disposition made under paragraph 672.54(b) or (c) be suspended pending the determination of the appeal;

(c) where the application of a disposition is suspended pursuant to section 672.75 or paragraph (b), make any other disposition in respect of the accused that is appropriate in the circumstances, other than a disposition under paragraph 672.54(a) or section 672.58, pending the determination of the appeal;

(d) where the application of a placement decision is suspended pursuant to an order made under paragraph (b), make any other placement decision that is appropriate in the circumstances, pending the determination of the appeal; and

(e) give any directions that the judge considers necessary for expediting the appeal.

CASELAW

THE PURPOSE OF SECTION 672.76

***Penetanguishene Mental Health Centre v. Ontario (Attorney General)*, [2001] O.J. No. 1074 (C.A.)**—At para. 7:

> [Section] 672.76's main purpose is to suspend dispositions in light of changes in circumstances which may, pending an appeal, make compliance with the earlier disposition inappropriate. This view of s. 672.76 accords with the present tense language of the section which focuses on the mental condition of the accused at the time of the motion. Before suspending a disposition, the court must be satisfied that the mental condition of the accused justifies it (s. 672.76(2)). The burden of persuasion lies with the moving party, in this case the hospital Administrators and the order is discretionary.

THE TEST REQUIRED TO INVOKE SECTION 672.76

***Waypoint Centre for Mental Health Care v. R.*, 2014 ONCA 182**—At para. 24, the court commented that "the test for suspending a placement decision pending appeal should be substantially the same as the test for suspending a disposition pending appeal."

***Northeast Mental Health Centre v. Rogers*, 2007 ONCA 561**—Section 672.76 is not limited to "changes in circumstances." The focus of the inquiry is the mental condition of the accused.[178] At para. 17: "motions under s. 672.76 should only be granted in extraordinary or rare circumstances; there must be compelling evidence adduced by the moving party that demonstrates that the Board's decision—given the mental condition of the accused person—is unsound or invalid; and, the onus is on the moving party to establish these necessary requirements." The hearing judge deciding an application under section 672.76 must do so in the context of the whole of Part XX.1, giving consideration to the mental condition of the accused, the protection of the public, the facili-

178 *Northeast Mental Health Centre v. Rogers*, 2007 ONCA 561 at para. 11.

tation of the treatment of the accused person, the requirement to restrict the accused's liberty as little as possible, and the authority of the Board to make binding orders.[179]

***Conway v. Brockville Psychiatric Hospital* (1994), 18 O.R. (3d) 27 (C.A.)**—Section 672.76 of the *Criminal Code* grants the Court of Appeal the authority to "relieve against a board disposition pending appeal where it is in the best interest of the accused having regard to his mental condition."[180] This section should be invoked only in extraordinary circumstances. The onus is on the applicant. The applicant must demonstrate that there are compelling reasons to doubt the validity or soundness of the disposition made by the Review Board as it related to the applicant's mental condition.

CASE EXAMPLES

***Waypoint Centre for Mental Health Care v. R.*, 2014 ONCA 182**[181]—The accused was a dual status offender and the Waypoint Centre for Mental Health Care brought a motion for an order suspending the placement decision of the Review Board, seeking an order that the accused remain in prison pending Waypoint's appeal of the Board's decision. The Board had ordered that the accused be transferred back to Waypoint after hearing expert evidence at a placement hearing. The Board was unanimous that the accused remained a significant threat to the safety of the public and that only a disposition of detention at a maximum-security hospital would be adequate to protect the public and meet the accused's treatment needs. The Court of Appeal dismissed Waypoint's motion as Waypoint did not persuade the court that compelling reasons existed to justify suspending the Board's decision. The Court of Appeal ordered that Waypoint's appeal of the Board's decision be expedited. The issue on appeal would be whether the Board lacked jurisdiction to make the placement decision.

***Furlan, Re*, 2013 ONCA 618**[182]—An application by the Crown for an order suspending an absolute discharge and directing the application of a conditional discharge pending appeal was granted on the basis of fresh evidence that the accused stopped taking his prescribed medication and began drinking and using drugs only weeks after the absolute discharge was granted. The fresh evidence demonstrated that the accused once again represented a threat to public safety due to his mental disorder. The proposed conditional discharge was the least onerous and least restrictive disposition.

***Northeast Mental Health Centre v. Rogers*, 2007 ONCA 561**—The Northeast Mental Health Centre's (NEMHC) motion to suspend the Board's order that the NCR accused be detained at the NEMHC medium-security facility—rather than a maximum-security facility—was dismissed. NEMHC failed to demonstrate extraordinary circumstances or compelling reasons to doubt the soundness of the Board's decision as it related to the accused's mental condition. The Board unanimously found the accused posed a significant risk to the safety of the public but did not require detention in a maximum-security facility.

* * * * *

179 *Ibid.* at para. 15.

180 *Conway*, above note 174 at para. 9.

181 At footnote 1 of its judgment, the court notes that the principle from *Penetanguishene Mental Health Centre v. Ontario (Attorney General)*, [2001] O.J. No. 1074 (C.A.) that a disposition may be suspended pending appeal when a change in circumstances makes compliance with the disposition inappropriate has no application in the motion before the court as there has been no change in circumstances since the Board's placement decision.

182 This case follows the principles set out in *Conway*, above note 174; *Northeast Mental Health Centre v. Rogers*, 2007 ONCA 561; and *Penetanguishene Mental Health Centre v. Ontario (Attorney General)*, [2001] O.J. No. 1074 (C.A.).

Copy of order to parties

(3) A judge of the court of appeal who makes an order under this section shall send a copy of the order to each of the parties without delay.

1991, c. 43, s. 4; 2014, c. 6, s. 14

Effect of suspension of disposition

672.77 Where the application of a disposition or placement decision appealed from is suspended, a disposition, or in the absence of a disposition any order for the interim release or detention of the accused, that was in effect immediately before the disposition or placement decision appealed from took effect, shall be in force pending the determination of the appeal, subject to any disposition made under paragraph 672.76(2)(c).

1991, c. 43, s. 4

Powers of court of appeal

672.78 (1) The court of appeal may allow an appeal against a disposition or placement decision and set aside an order made by the court or Review Board, where the court of appeal is of the opinion that

(a) it is unreasonable or cannot be supported by the evidence;
(b) it is based on a wrong decision on a question of law; or
(c) there was a miscarriage of justice.

CASELAW

STANDARD OF REVIEW

***Canada (Minister of Citizenship and Immigration) v. Vavilov*, 2019 SCC 65**—Properly appreciating the evidence is related to whether the resulting decision is reasonable and "[t]he reasonableness of a decision may be jeopardized where the decision maker has fundamentally misapprehended or failed to account for the evidence before it."[183] Reasonableness "'is concerned mostly with the existence of justification, transparency and intelligibility within the decision-making process', as well as 'with whether the decision falls within a range of possible, acceptable outcomes which are defensible in respect of the facts and law': *ibid.* In short, it is not enough for the outcome of a decision to be *justifiable*."[184]

***R. v. Palmer*, 2013 ONCA 475**—At para. 30, it states that "the court must take a functional, substantive approach and have regard to the evidentiary record when it is reviewing the adequacy of the Board's reasons."[185]

***Saikaley, Re*, 2012 ONCA 92**—A Board's disposition, if within the range of reasonable outcomes supported by the evidence, is entitled to deference. In this case, S.E. Lang J.A. provides a helpful summary of the relevant, governing caselaw:

> 34 The standard of review was not a matter of controversy. Section 672.78(1) of the *Criminal Code* provides that an appeal may only be allowed if a Board order is unreasonable or cannot be supported by the evidence, is based on a wrong decision on a question of law, or gives rise to a miscarriage of justice.

---

183 *Canada (Minister of Citizenship and Immigration) v. Vavilov*, 2019 SCC 65 at para. 126.

184 *Ibid.* at para. 86, citing *Dunsmuir v. New Brunswick*, 2008 SCC 9.

185 The court cites *R. v. M. (R.E.)*, 2008 SCC 51 at paras. 16 and 35.

35 The Supreme Court of Canada has instructed appellate courts not to "be too quick to overturn a review board's 'expert opinion' on how best to manage a patient's risk to the public" (citations omitted): *R. v. Conway*, 2010 SCC 22, [2010] 1 S.C.R. 765 (S.C.C.), at para 95. However, the Board's risk assessment and disposition can be considered unreasonable when not "'supported by reasons that can bear even a somewhat probing examination'": *Mazzei v. British Columbia (Director of Adult Forensic Psychiatric Services)*, 2006 SCC 7, [2006] 1 S.C.R. 326 (S.C.C.), at para. 17.

36 Deference will generally be accorded to a tribunal's interpretation of its home statute or statutes that are "closely connected to its function", and may also be warranted where a tribunal has developed expertise in applying a general rule of common or civil law in specific statutory contexts: *New Brunswick (Board of Management) v. Dunsmuir*, 2008 SCC 9, [2008] 1 S.C.R. 190 (S.C.C.), at para. 54. Correctness is the appropriate standard of review for constitutional questions, particularly questions of *Charter* interpretation: see *Barrie Public Utilities v. Canadian Cable Television Assn.*, 2003 SCC 28, [2003] 1 S.C.R. 476 (S.C.C.), at para. 66 and *K Mart Canada Ltd. v. U.F.C.W., Local 1518*, [1999] 2 S.C.R. 1083 (S.C.C.), at paras. 69-70. However, where the question is one of discretion, deference usually applies automatically: see *Dunsmuir*, at para. 53. The determination of an appropriate s. 24(1) *Charter* remedy generally involves an exercise of discretion: *R. v. Carosella*, [1997] 1 S.C.R. 80 (S.C.C.), at para. 48.

***Manitoba (Attorney General) v. Singer*, 2006 MBCA 64, leave to appeal to S.C.C. dismissed 2006 CarswellMan 412**—The standard of review of the Board's decision is one of reasonableness.

***Penetanguishene Mental Health Centre v. Magee*, [2006] O.J. No. 1926 (C.A.)**—In this case, Cronk J.A. provides a helpful summary of the relevant, governing caselaw with respect to the standard of review (paras. 51–52). The first branch of section 672.78 imports a reasonableness standard of review.[186] This standard recognizes a review board's expertise in mental health disorders and attendant safety risks, its specialized knowledge and advantage in observing witnesses, and its familiarity with the situation of a specific NCR accused based upon its annual review of the status of each NCR individual under section 672.81(1) of the *Code*. These factors require deference to a review board's risk assessment of an NCR accused and its disposition order.[187] The second branch of the section 672.78 power of appellate review concerns a wrong decision on a question of law, which attracts the correctness standard of review.[188]

***Pinet v. St. Thomas Psychiatric Hospital*, 2004 SCC 21**—The Review Board did not accept that the conditions of the appellant's continued detention were required by section 672.54 of the *Criminal Code* to be "the least onerous and least restrictive" of the appellant's liberty after taking into consideration the other factors in that section.[189] Unlike *Owen* (below), the Review Board's decision in this case proceeded on the basis of an error of law and the Review Board used its expertise to structure a disposition order that rested on a faulty legal foundation.[190] This case was decided under the second branch of the power of appellate review under section 672.78(1)(b). When an error of law has been established by the appellant, the onus shifts to the respondent Crown to attempt to salvage the Review Board order on the basis that no "substantial wrong" was done.[191] The reference to no "substantial wrong" in section 672.78 requires the party seeking to uphold the order (here it is the Crown) to satisfy the appellate court that a Review Board, acting reasonably,

186 The court cites *Owen*, above note 113 at paras. 33 and 34 and *Mazzei*, above note 98 at para. 17.

187 The court cites *Owen*, above note 113 at paras. 29–30 and 36–37 and *Winko*, above note 100 at para. 61.

188 The court cites *Mazzei*, above note 98 at para. 16; *Penetanguishene Mental Health Centre v. Ontario (Attorney General)*, [2004] 1 S.C.R. 498 (also referred to as *Tulikorpi*); and *Pinet*, below note 187 at paras. 24–29.

189 *Pinet v. St. Thomas Psychiatric Hospital*, 2004 SCC 21 at para. 23 [*Pinet*].

190 *Ibid.* at para. 23.

191 *Ibid.* at para. 25.

and properly informed of the law, would necessarily have reached the same conclusion absent the legal error.[192] The onus was not satisfied by the respondent Crown nor the respondent administrator of St. Thomas Psychiatric Hospital; the court could therefore not say no substantial wrong was done. The appellant was entitled to a rehearing.

***R. v. Owen*, 2003 SCC 33**—The standard of review of a disposition or placement decision of the Board by the Ontario Court of Appeal is set out in section 672.78(1) of the *Criminal Code*; the Board's decision is reviewable on a reasonableness standard. A reviewing court can only set aside an order of the Board where it is of the opinion that the decision is unreasonable or cannot be supported by the evidence; it is based on a wrong decision on a question of law; or there was a miscarriage of justice.[193] The Board's reasons must be able to withstand a "somewhat probing examination."[194] The assessment and expertise of the Board attracts considerable deference—owing to the expertise of the Board—so long as the conditions of detention lie within a range of reasonable judgment. The Board's decision must fall within a range of reasonable outcomes. Note that this case was decided under the first branch of the power of appellate review under section 672.78(1)(a). Also see ***Hart, Re*, 2016 ONCA 277 at para. 6.**

RETURN OF MATTER TO REVIEW BOARD

***Nadery, Re*, 2011 ONCA 573**—Pursuant to section 672.78(1) of the *Criminal* Code, the Court of Appeal has the power to refer a matter back to the Board for a rehearing "in whole or in part, in accordance with any directions that the Court of Appeal considers appropriate." Once the matter is remitted back to the Board to determine appropriate conditions (as ordered in this case, with the Court of Appeal ordering a conditional discharge), it is an error of law for the Board to conclude that it is entitled to engage in a full scale review of the accused's situation, including: (1) declining to comply with the Court of Appeal's order to impose a conditional discharge; and (2) ordering the delay of an accused's annual review. In this case, the Board's action was contrary to the order of the Court of Appeal, denied procedural fairness to the appellant as he was not on notice that such a hearing would be held, and denied the appellant the right to a mandatory annual review pursuant to section 672.81 of the *Criminal Code.*

* * * * *

Idem

(2) The court of appeal may dismiss an appeal against a disposition or placement decision where the court is of the opinion

(a) that paragraphs (1)(a), (b) and (c) do not apply; or

(b) that paragraph (1)(b) may apply, but the court finds that no substantial wrong or miscarriage of justice has occurred.

Orders that the court may make

(3) Where the court of appeal allows an appeal against a disposition or placement decision, it may

(a) make any disposition under section 672.54 or any placement decision that the Review Board could have made;

(b) refer the matter back to the court or Review Board for re-hearing, in whole or in part, in accordance with any directions that the court of appeal considers appropriate; or

(c) make any other order that justice requires.

1991, c. 43, s. 4; 1997, c. 18, s. 89

192 *Ibid.* at para. 28.

193 See paras. 31–37.

194 *Owen*, above note 113 at para. 33.

672.79 [Repealed, 2005, c. 22, s. 26]

672.8 [Repealed, 2005, c. 22, s. 26]

Review of Dispositions

Mandatory review of dispositions

672.81 (1) A Review Board shall hold a hearing not later than twelve months after making a disposition and every twelve months thereafter for as long as the disposition remains in force, to review any disposition that it has made in respect of an accused, other than an absolute discharge under paragraph 672.54(a).

CASELAW

***Martin v. British Columbia (Director of Adult Forensic Psychiatric Services)* (2000) (*sub nom. Martin, Re*) 2000 CarswellBC 1226 (C.A.), leave to appeal to S.C.C. refused [2000] S.C.C.A. No. 412, 2001 CarswellBC 322**—Where missing or failing to abide by a statutory time limit causes no prejudice to the accused, the Board does not lose jurisdiction over the accused.

See also ***Doucet v. British Columbia (Director of Adult Forensic Psychiatric Services)*, 2000 BCCA 195** for a similar decision involving the requirement under section 672.47(1) to hold an initial Board hearing within forty-five days of the verdict of NCRMD. The majority held that failing to abide by the forty-five-day time limit without demonstrating substantial prejudice did not result in loss of jurisdiction.

* * * * *

Extension on consent

(1.1) Despite subsection (1), the Review Board may extend the time for holding a hearing to a maximum of twenty-four months after the making or reviewing of a disposition if the accused is represented by counsel and the accused and the Attorney General consent to the extension.

Extension for serious personal violence offence

(1.2) Despite subsection (1), at the conclusion of a hearing under this section the Review Board may, after making a disposition, extend the time for holding a subsequent hearing under this section to a maximum of twenty-four months if

(a) the accused has been found not criminally responsible for a serious personal injury offence;

(b) the accused is subject to a disposition made under paragraph 672.54(c); and

(c) the Review Board is satisfied on the basis of any relevant information, including disposition information within the meaning of subsection 672.51(1) and an assessment report made under an assessment ordered under paragraph 672.121(a), that the condition of the accused is not likely to improve and that detention remains necessary for the period of the extension.

Definition of serious personal injury offence

(1.3) For the purposes of subsection (1.2), serious personal injury offence means

(a) an indictable offence involving

(i) the use or attempted use of violence against another person, or

(ii) conduct endangering or likely to endanger the life or safety of another person or inflicting or likely to inflict severe psychological damage upon another person; or

(b) an indictable offence referred to in section 151, 152, 153, 153.1, 155, 160, 170, 171, 172, 271, 272 or 273 or an attempt to commit such an offence.

Extension on consent—high-risk accused

(1.31) Despite subsections (1) to (1.2), the Review Board may extend the time for holding a hearing in respect of a high-risk accused to a maximum of 36 months after making or reviewing a disposition if the accused is represented by counsel and the accused and the Attorney General consent to the extension.

Extension—no likely improvement

(1.32) Despite subsections (1) to (1.2), at the conclusion of a hearing under subsection 672.47(4) or this section in respect of a high-risk accused, the Review Board may, after making a disposition, extend the time for holding a subsequent hearing under this section to a maximum of 36 months if the Review Board is satisfied on the basis of any relevant information, including disposition information as defined in subsection 672.51(1) and an assessment report made under an assessment ordered under paragraph 672.121(c), that the accused's condition is not likely to improve and that detention remains necessary for the period of the extension.

Notice

(1.4) If the Review Board extends the time for holding a hearing under subsection (1.2) or (1.32), it shall provide notice of the extension to the accused, the prosecutor and the person in charge of the hospital where the accused is detained.

Appeal

(1.5) A decision by the Review Board to extend the time for holding a hearing under subsection (1.2) or (1.32) is deemed to be a disposition for the purpose of sections 672.72 to 672.78.

Additional mandatory reviews in custody cases

(2) The Review Board shall hold a hearing to review any disposition made under paragraph 672.54(b) or (c) as soon as practicable after receiving notice that the person in charge of the place where the accused is detained or directed to attend requests the review.

CASELAW

***Katzav, Re*, 2013 ONCA 627**— It is not an abuse of the ORB's process for the hospital to seek the early review contemplated in section 672.81(2) (see para. 14).

*****

Review in case of increase on restrictions on liberty

(2.1) The Review Board shall hold a hearing to review a decision to significantly increase the restrictions on the liberty of the accused, as soon as practicable after receiving the notice referred to in subsection 672.56(2).

CASELAW

PURPOSE

***Campbell, Re*, 2018 ONCA 140** — At para. 64, "the purpose of s. 672.56(2) is to act as a final liberty safeguard, allowing for a second-look at those hospital decisions that have such serious ramifications for the liberty of the NCR accused, that they should be examined ahead of the next yearly review."

NOTICE

***Heinekamp, Re*, 2024 ONCA 183** — The hospital is required to give notice to the Board of any increase in restrictions on the appellant's liberty to ensure a restriction on liberty hearing can be held "as soon as practicable."[195]

TIMING: MEANING OF "AS SOON AS PRACTICABLE"

***Saikaley, Re*, 2012 ONCA 92**—There is no evidence to conclude that "as soon as practicable" under section 672.81(2.1) means that a restriction hearing should be held within thirty days from the date that notice is received. Hearings and decisions to which patients are entitled should be rendered "as expeditiously as is practicable."[196] Parliament did not impose a set time frame and instead used the flexible language of "as soon as practicable." Parliament clearly intended that restriction hearing should be set, held, and concluded expeditiously. Where a patient's liberty has been significantly restricted, an expeditious hearing provides an important safeguard.[197] The Board did not err in leaving the particulars of implementation to the institutions, particularly in light of the myriad available options.[198]

***Re Starz* (2015), 324 C.C.C. (3d) 228 (Ont. C.A.)**—Failure of the Board to hold a hearing within the time stipulated by the statute does not necessarily constitute a section 7 *Charter* violation.

CONFINEMENT UNDER CIVIL MENTAL HEALTH LEGISLATION NOT A RESTRICTION OF LIBERTY

***Centre of Addiction and Mental Health v. Young* (2011), 273 C.C.C. (3d) 512 (Ont. C.A.)**—An accused's confinement pursuant to the provisions of civil mental health legislation does not constitute a restriction of liberty as contemplated by section 672.56.

* * * * *

Idem

(3) Where an accused is detained in custody pursuant to a disposition made under paragraph 672.54(c) and a sentence of imprisonment is subsequently imposed on the accused in respect of another offence, the Review Board shall hold a hearing to review the disposition as soon as is practicable after receiving notice of that sentence.

1991, c. 43, s. 4; 2005, c. 22, ss. 27, 42(F); 2014, c. 6, s. 15

Discretionary review

672.82 (1) A Review Board may hold a hearing to review any of its dispositions at any time, of its own motion or at the request of the accused or any other party.

Review Board to provide notice

(1.1) Where a Review Board holds a hearing under subsection (1) of its own motion, it shall provide notice to the prosecutor, the accused and any other party.

---

195 *Heinekamp, Re*, 2024 ONCA 183 at para. 25.

196 *Saikaley, Re*, 2012 ONCA 92 at para. 72.

197 *Ibid.* at para. 68.

198 *Ibid.* at para. 71. The court cites the following cases: *Mahe v. Alberta*, [1990] 1 S.C.R. 342 at 393; *Eldridge v. British Columbia (Attorney General)*, [1997] 3 S.C.R. 624 at para. 96.

Review cancels appeal

(2) Where a party requests a review of a disposition under this section, the party is deemed to abandon any appeal against the disposition taken under section 672.72.

1991, c. 43, s. 4; 2005, c. 22, s. 28

Disposition by Review Board

672.83 (1) At a hearing held pursuant to section 672.81 or 672.82, the Review Board shall, except where a determination is made under subsection 672.48(1) that the accused is fit to stand trial, review the disposition made in respect of the accused and make any other disposition that the Review Board considers to be appropriate in the circumstances.

(2) [Repealed, 2005, c. 22, s. 29]

1991, c. 43, s. 4; 1997, c. 18, s. 90; 2005, c. 22, ss. 29, 42(F)

Review of finding—high-risk accused

672.84 (1) If a Review Board holds a hearing under section 672.81 or 672.82 in respect of a high-risk accused, it shall, on the basis of any relevant information, including disposition information as defined in subsection 672.51(1) and an assessment report made under an assessment ordered under paragraph 672.121(c), if it is satisfied that there is not a substantial likelihood that the accused—whether found to be a high-risk accused under paragraph 672.64(1)(a) or (b) — will use violence that could endanger the life or safety of another person, refer the finding for review to the superior court of criminal jurisdiction.

Review of conditions

(2) If the Review Board is not so satisfied, it shall review the conditions of detention imposed under paragraph 672.54(c), subject to the restrictions set out in subsection 672.64(3).

Review of finding by court

(3) If the Review Board refers the finding to the superior court of criminal jurisdiction for review, the court shall, at the conclusion of a hearing, revoke the finding if the court is satisfied that there is not a substantial likelihood that the accused will use violence that could endanger the life or safety of another person, in which case the court or the Review Board shall make a disposition under any of paragraphs 672.54(a) to (c).

Hearing and disposition

(4) Any disposition referred to in subsection (3) is subject to sections 672.45 to 672.47 as if the revocation is a verdict.

Review of conditions

(5) If the court does not revoke the finding, it shall immediately send to the Review Board, in original or copied form, a transcript of the hearing, any other document or information related to the hearing, and all exhibits filed with it, if the transcript, document, information or exhibits are in its possession. The Review Board shall, as soon as practicable but not later than 45 days after the day on which the court decides not to revoke the finding, hold a hearing and review the conditions of detention imposed under paragraph 672.54(c), subject to the restrictions set out in subsection 672.64(3).

Appeal

(6) A decision under subsection (1) about referring the finding to the court for review and a decision under subsection (3) about revoking the finding are deemed to be dispositions for the purpose of sections 672.72 to 672.78.

1991, c. 43, s. 4; 2005, c. 22, s. 30; 2014, c. 6, s. 16

Power to Compel Appearance

Bringing accused before Review Board

672.85 For the purpose of bringing the accused in respect of whom a hearing is to be held before the Review Board, including in circumstances in which the accused did not attend a previous hearing in contravention of a summons or warrant, the chairperson

(a) shall order the person having custody of the accused to bring the accused to the hearing at the time and place fixed for it; or

(b) may, if the accused is not in custody, issue a summons or warrant to compel the accused to appear at the hearing at the time and place fixed for it.

1991, c. 43, s. 4; 2005, c. 22, ss. 32, 42(F)

Stay of Proceedings

Recommendation by Review Board

672.851 (1) The Review Board may, of its own motion, make a recommendation to the court that has jurisdiction in respect of the offence charged against an accused found unfit to stand trial to hold an inquiry to determine whether a stay of proceedings should be ordered if

(a) the Review Board has held a hearing under section 672.81 or 672.82 in respect of the accused; and

(b) on the basis of any relevant information, including disposition information within the meaning of subsection 672.51(1) and an assessment report made under an assessment ordered under paragraph 672.121(a), the Review Board is of the opinion that

(i) the accused remains unfit to stand trial and is not likely to ever become fit to stand trial, and

(ii) the accused does not pose a significant threat to the safety of the public.

Notice

(2) If the Review Board makes a recommendation to the court to hold an inquiry, the Review Board shall provide notice to the accused, the prosecutor and any party who, in the opinion of the Review Board, has a substantial interest in protecting the interests of the accused.

Inquiry

(3) As soon as practicable after receiving the recommendation referred to in subsection (1), the court may hold an inquiry to determine whether a stay of proceedings should be ordered.

Court may act on own motion

(4) A court may, of its own motion, conduct an inquiry to determine whether a stay of proceedings should be ordered if the court is of the opinion, on the basis of any relevant information, that

(a) the accused remains unfit to stand trial and is not likely to ever become fit to stand trial; and

(b) the accused does not pose a significant threat to the safety of the public.

Assessment order

(5) If the court holds an inquiry under subsection (3) or (4), it shall order an assessment of the accused.

Application

(6) Section 672.51 applies to an inquiry of the court under this section.

Stay

(7) The court may, on completion of an inquiry under this section, order a stay of proceedings if it is satisfied

(a) on the basis of clear information, that the accused remains unfit to stand trial and is not likely to ever become fit to stand trial;

(b) that the accused does not pose a significant threat to the safety of the public; and

(c) that a stay is in the interests of the proper administration of justice.

Proper administration of justice

(8) In order to determine whether a stay of proceedings is in the interests of the proper administration of justice, the court shall consider any submissions of the prosecutor, the accused and all other parties and the following factors:

(a) the nature and seriousness of the alleged offence;

(b) the salutary and deleterious effects of the order for a stay of proceedings, including any effect on public confidence in the administration of justice;

(c) the time that has elapsed since the commission of the alleged offence and whether an inquiry has been held under section 672.33 to decide whether sufficient evidence can be adduced to put the accused on trial; and

(d) any other factor that the court considers relevant.

Effect of stay

(9) If a stay of proceedings is ordered by the court, any disposition made in respect of the accused ceases to have effect. If a stay of proceedings is not ordered, the finding of unfit to stand trial and any disposition made in respect of the accused remain in force, until the Review Board holds a disposition hearing and makes a disposition in respect of the accused under section 672.83.

2005, c. 22, s. 33

SECTION SUMMARY

Sections 672.851(1) to 672.851(9) allow the Review Board to conduct an inquiry into whether a stay of proceedings should be ordered. The court may act on its own motion to conduct such an inquiry. If the Review Board makes a recommendation that such an inquiry should be held, the Review Board must provide notice to the accused, the prosecutor, and any party who has a substantial interest in protecting the interests of the accused. Once the inquiry is completed, the court may order a stay of proceedings if it is satisfied that the accused remains unfit to stand trial and is not likely to ever become fit to stand trial, that the accused does not pose a significant threat to the safety of the public, and that a stay is in the interests of the proper administration of justice. The factors that the court shall consider to determine if a stay is in the interests of the proper administration of justice are found in section 672.851(8).

HISTORICAL BACKGROUND

***R. v. Demers*, [2004] 2 S.C.R. 489**—The failure of Parliament to provide for the possibility of an absolute discharge for an accused who is permanently unfit and not dangerous violates section 7 of the *Charter* because it is overbroad. Part XX.1 did not treat fairly permanently unfit accused that are not a significant threat for public safety. The scheme did not provide for the end of the prosecution. The declaration of invalidity was suspended for twelve months to give Parliament a chance to act. Parliament revised the legislation, resulting in section 672.851. The current legislation permits a judicial stay of proceedings where certain conditions are satisfied, including that the accused is permanently unfit to stand trial, is not likely to ever become fit, and is not a significant threat to the safety of the public.

Commentary: With the proclamation of Bill C-10 on 19 May 2005, the court's new ability to stay proceedings in respect of a permanently unfit accused under Part XX.1 of the *Criminal Code* came into effect on 30 June 2005. Prior to the proclamation of Bill C-10, an unfit accused would remain subject to the jurisdiction of the Review Board indefinitely, so long as they remained unfit to stand trial (unless the Crown failed to show a *prima facie* case within every two years post-verdict: section 672.33). Jurisdiction over the accused was not dangerousness-based (as is the case for accused found to be NCR). Where the "mental disorder" mediating the unfitness was intellectual disability, brain injury, or some other intractable condition, the accused could remain subject to the jurisdiction of the Review Board forever. This situation was frustrating both for the accused and the Review Board which had no ability to discharge the accused as it might if the accused were NCR. Stays, where entered, were the result of the Crown exercising its discretion on an *ad hoc* basis.

CONSTITUTIONALITY

Section 672.851(1) permits a Review Board to recommend to the court that it hold an inquiry to determine whether a stay of proceedings should be ordered if, in the Board's opinion, an accused is unfit and not likely to ever become fit, and does not pose a significant threat to the safety of the public. This power is, however, limited in section 672.851(1)(a); and the Review Board cannot make such a recommendation when considering the case for the first time (specifically, at a disposition hearing under section 672.47). In ***R. v. Lynn*, 2020 ONSC 4581**, the Ontario Superior Court upheld the constitutionality of section 672.851(1)(a) of the *Criminal Code*, finding no section 7 *Charter* breach resulted from the Review Board being unable to recommend, at an initial disposition hearing, to a court that it hold an inquiry to determine whether a stay of proceedings should be ordered if, in the Board's opinion, an accused is unfit and not likely to ever become fit, and does not pose a significant threat to the safety of the public.

RELATED PROVISIONS

Section 672.851(5) sets out that the court holding a stay inquiry *shall* order an assessment of the accused if it holds a stay inquiry. The court's discretionary ability to order an assessment under section 672.11 is specifically contemplated in the circumstances of a stay under section 672.11(e): "A court having jurisdiction over an accused in respect of an offence may order an assessment of the mental condition of the accused, if it has reasonable grounds to believe that such evidence is necessary to determine whether an order should be made under section 672.851 for a stay of proceedings where a verdict of unfit to stand trial has been rendered against the accused."

Section 672.852(1)–(2) provides for the opportunity to appeal against an order for a stay of proceedings, if the Court of Appeal is of the opinion that the order is unreasonable or cannot be supported by the evidence.

CASELAW

PRESUMPTION

***Banks, Re*, 2006 CarswellOnt 8525 (*sub nom. G.B., Re*), [2006] O.R.B.D. No. 37 (Ont. Review Bd.)**—A recommendation pursuant to section 672.851 presupposes that the unfit accused does not pose a significant threat to the safety of the public.

***R. v. Demers*, [2004] 2 S.C.R. 489**—A permanently unfit accused, who does not constitute a significant threat to the safety of the public, should be treated the same as the NCR accused who does not pose a significant threat to the safety of the public. There should be a route available for a stay of proceedings to be ordered for the permanently unfit accused. The permanently unfit accused is still presumed to be innocent, whereas, in contrast, there has been a finding of guilt in respect of the NCR accused.

Note: This case led to the creation of the stay provisions as they exist today. **See above, "Historical Background."**

BOARD'S INABILITY TO RECOMMEND A STAY AT THE INITIAL DISPOSITION HEARING DOES NOT VIOLATE SECTION 7 OF THE *CHARTER*

***R. v. Lynn*, 2020 ONSC 4581**—The Ontario Superior Court upheld the constitutionality of section 672.851(1)(a) of the *Criminal Code*, finding no section 7 *Charter* breach resulted from the Review Board being unable to recommend, at an initial disposition hearing, to a court that it hold an inquiry to determine whether a stay of proceedings should be ordered if, in the Board's opinion, an accused is unfit and not likely to ever become fit, and does not pose a significant threat to the safety of the public.

PROCEDURE AND EVIDENTIARY BURDEN

***R. v. Kearly*, [2005] O.J. No. 5394 (C.J.)**—An inquiry pursuant to the provisions of section 672.851 would, as much as possible, be carried out in the same manner as a hearing pursuant to the provisions of section 672.54. To a large extent, the Supreme Court of Canada's rulings in *Winko* are applicable. At para. 13, those key provisions from *Kearly* are as follows:

1) There is to be no presumption that the mentally disordered accused poses a significant threat to the safety of the public,
2) The accused is never in a position of having to disprove dangerousness—the accused is therefore relieved of any legal or evidentiary burden—the accused need do nothing (unless, of course, dangerousness is otherwise established),
3) This tactical incentive to adduce evidence is not properly described as a shifting of the legal or evidentiary burden to the accused,
4) If the court or Review Board is unable to conclude that the accused constitutes a significant threat to the safety of the public, he or she must be absolutely discharged,
5) Jurisdiction over the accused cannot be maintained where there is doubt regarding dangerousness, continued jurisdiction requires an affirmative finding of significant threat,
6) The threat posed must be more than speculative in nature; it must be supported by the evidence,
7) The threat must also be "significant", both in the sense that there must be a real risk of physical or psychological harm occurring to individuals in the community and in the sense that this potential harm be serious. A miniscule risk of a grave harm will not suffice. Similarly, a high risk of trivial harm will not meet the threshold,
8) The conduct or activity creating the harm must be criminal in nature,
9) Finally, it is up to the court or Review Board to ensure that it has sufficient information in order to make the determination.

EXAMPLE OF A STAY BEING RECOMMENDED BY A REVIEW BOARD

***Birdsell, Re*, 2013 CarswellOnt 716 (Ont. Review. Bd.)**—In the context of a hospitalized geriatric unfit accused with no violent history other than the index offence and aggressive but explainable events shortly thereafter, the Review Board recommended a stay of proceedings to the court.

EXAMPLE OF A STAY BEING ORDERED BY A COURT OF APPEAL

***L. (R.) v. R.*, 2017 QCCS 6376**—Upon the earlier decision from the Court of Appeal in this matter finding, *inter alia*, that an accused had to be fit to stand trial in order to have a bail hearing, the Superior Court granted the accused's application for a stay of proceedings as a result of the "Kafkaesque procedural nightmare" experienced by the accused.[199] The accused, who suffers from a mental disorder, was in custody for more than four years without a bail hearing while the matter of his fitness to stand trial remained outstanding. The petitioner's detention in two different prisons while waiting for his second fitness hearing violated his section 7 *Charter* right. Neither prison was a "hospital" defined by the *Code*.[200]

EXAMPLE OF A STAY BEING INAPPROPRIATE WHERE NCR VERDICT FOUND IN ERROR

***R. v. A. (P.)*, 2011 ONCA 673**—A mentally ill Indigenous youth entered a guilty plea to one count of breaking and entering with intent to commit an indictable offence. The trial judge accepted the plea, and the Crown sought a finding of NCRMD, leading to an NCR hearing where the accused was found NCR and detained at the Mental Health Centre Penetanguishene—Oak Ridge Division. The accused's appeal was allowed, and the NCR verdict was set aside as the appellant's plea and NCR hearing were rife with reversible errors. The extraordinary remedy of a stay is not appropriate in this case. A stay is only justified in the clearest of cases, where no other remedy is available.[201] Based on the appellant's fresh acknowledgement of guilt, a conviction to one count of breaking and entering with intent was entered and a sentence of a one-day imprisonment was imposed.[202]

* * * * *

Appeal

672.852 (1) The Court of Appeal may allow an appeal against an order made under subsection 672.851(7) for a stay of proceedings, if the Court of Appeal is of the opinion that the order is unreasonable or cannot be supported by the evidence.

Effect

(2) If the Court of Appeal allows the appeal, it may set aside the order for a stay of proceedings and restore the finding that the accused is unfit to stand trial and the disposition made in respect of the accused.

2005, c. 22, s. 33

Interprovincial Transfers

Interprovincial transfers

672.86 (1) An accused who is detained in custody or directed to attend at a hospital pursuant to a disposition made by a court or Review Board under paragraph 672.54(c) or a court under section 672.58 may be transferred to any other place in Canada where

(a) the Review Board of the province where the accused is detained or directed to attend recommends a transfer for the purpose of the reintegration of the accused into society or the recovery, treatment or custody of the accused; and

---

199 *L. (R.) v. R.*, 2017 QCCS 6376 at para. 1.

200 *Ibid.* at para. 89. Content reproduced in part and repurposed with permission from *Fitness to Stand Trial*, above note 12 at Appendix A, 199.

201 The court cites *R. v. Jewitt*, [1985] 2 S.C.R. 128 at 136–37; *R. v. O'Connor*, [1995] 4 S.C.R. 411 at para 82.

202 *R. v. A. (P.)*, 2011 ONCA 673 at paras. 13–14. The appellant had been in custody for approximately fifteen months.

(b) the Attorney General of the province to which the accused is being transferred, or an officer authorized by that Attorney General, and the Attorney General of the province from which the accused is being transferred, or an officer authorized by that Attorney General, give their consent.

Transfer where accused in custody

(2) Where an accused who is detained in custody is to be transferred, an officer authorized by the Attorney General of the province where the accused is being detained shall sign a warrant specifying the place in Canada to which the accused is to be transferred.

Transfer if accused not in custody

(2.1) An accused who is not detained in custody may be transferred to any other place in Canada where

(a) the Review Board of the province from which the accused is being transferred recommends a transfer for the purpose of the reintegration of the accused into society or the recovery or treatment of the accused; and

(b) the Attorney General of the province to which the accused is being transferred, or an officer authorized by that Attorney General, and the Attorney General of the province from which the accused is being transferred, or an officer authorized by that Attorney General, give their consent.

Order

(3) Where an accused is being transferred in accordance with subsection (2.1), the Review Board of the province from which the accused is being transferred shall, by order,

(a) direct that the accused be taken into custody and transferred pursuant to a warrant under subsection (2); or

(b) direct that the accused attend at a specified place in Canada, subject to any conditions that the Review Board of the province to or from which the accused is being transferred considers appropriate.

1991, c. 43, s. 4; 2005, c. 22, s. 34

Delivery and detention of accused

672.87 A warrant described in subsection 672.86(2) is sufficient authority

(a) for any person who is responsible for the custody of an accused to have the accused taken into custody and conveyed to the person in charge of the place specified in the warrant; and

(b) for the person specified in the warrant to detain the accused in accordance with any disposition made in respect of the accused under paragraph 672.54(c).

1991, c. 43, s. 4

Review Board of receiving province

672.88 (1) The Review Board of the province to which an accused is transferred under section 672.86 has exclusive jurisdiction over the accused, and may exercise the powers and shall perform the duties mentioned in sections 672.5 and 672.81 to 672.84 as if that Review Board had made the disposition in respect of the accused.

Agreement

(2) Notwithstanding subsection (1), the Attorney General of the province to which an accused is transferred may enter into an agreement subject to this Act with the Attorney General of the province from which the accused is transferred, enabling the Review Board of that province to exercise the powers and perform the duties referred to in subsection (1) in respect of the accused, in the circumstances and subject to the terms and conditions set out in the agreement.

1991, c. 43, s. 4; 2014, c. 6, s. 17

Other interprovincial transfers

672.89 (1) If an accused who is detained in custody under a disposition made by a Review Board is transferred to another province otherwise than under section 672.86, the Review Board of the province from which the accused is transferred has exclusive jurisdiction over the accused and may continue to exercise the powers and shall continue to perform the duties mentioned in sections 672.5 and 672.81 to 672.84.

Agreement

(2) Notwithstanding subsection (1), the Attorneys General of the provinces to and from which the accused is to be transferred as described in that subsection may, after the transfer is made, enter into an agreement subject to this Act, enabling the Review Board of the province to which an accused is transferred to exercise the powers and perform the duties referred to in subsection (1) in respect of the accused, subject to the terms and conditions and in the circumstances set out in the agreement.

1991, c. 43, s. 4; 2014, c. 6, s. 18

Enforcement of Orders and Regulations

Execution of warrant anywhere in Canada

672.9 Any warrant or process issued in relation to an assessment order or disposition made in respect of an accused may be executed or served in any place in Canada outside the province where the order or disposition was made as if it had been issued in that province.

1991, c. 43, s. 4; 1997, c. 18, s. 91; 2005, c. 22, s. 35(F)

Arrest without warrant for contravention of disposition

672.91 A peace officer may arrest an accused without a warrant at any place in Canada if the peace officer has reasonable grounds to believe that the accused has contravened or wilfully failed to comply with the assessment order or disposition or any condition of it, or is about to do so.

1991, c. 43, s. 4; 2005, c. 22, s. 36

Release or delivery of accused subject to paragraph 672.54(b) disposition order

672.92 (1) If a peace officer arrests an accused under section 672.91 who is subject to a disposition made under paragraph 672.54(b) or an assessment order, the peace officer, as soon as practicable, may release the accused from custody and

(a) issue a summons or appearance notice compelling the accused's appearance before a justice; and

(b) deliver the accused to the place specified in the disposition or assessment order.

No release

(2) A peace officer shall not release an accused under subsection (1) if the peace officer believes, on reasonable grounds,

(a) that it is necessary in the public interest that the accused be detained in custody having regard to all the circumstances, including the need to

  (i) establish the identity of the accused,

  (ii) establish the terms and conditions of a disposition made under section 672.54 or of an assessment order,

  (iii) prevent the commission of an offence, or

  (iv) prevent the accused from contravening or failing to comply with the disposition or assessment order;

(b) that the accused is subject to a disposition or an assessment order of a court, or Review Board, of another province; or

(c) that, if the accused is released from custody, the accused will fail to attend, as required, before a justice.

Accused to be brought before justice
(3) If a peace officer does not release the accused, the accused shall be taken before a justice having jurisdiction in the territorial division in which the accused is arrested, without unreasonable delay and in any event within twenty-four hours after the arrest.

Accused subject to paragraph 672.54(c) disposition order
(4) If a peace officer arrests an accused under section 672.91 who is subject to a disposition under paragraph 672.54(c), the accused shall be taken before a justice having jurisdiction in the territorial division in which the accused is arrested without unreasonable delay and, in any event, within twenty-four hours.

Justice not available
(5) If a justice described in subsection (3) or (4) is not available within twenty-four hours after the arrest, the accused shall be taken before a justice as soon as practicable.
1991, c. 43, s. 4; 2005, c. 22, s. 36

Where justice to release accused
672.93 (1) A justice shall release an accused who is brought before the justice under section 672.92 unless the justice is satisfied that there are reasonable grounds to believe that the accused has contravened or failed to comply with a disposition or an assessment order.

CASELAW

***R. v. Tenegu*, [2020] O.J. No. 4263 (S.C.J.)** — In the context of a bail review, the Superior Court of Justice does not have jurisdiction to review a justice's order that refers an accused to the Review Board under section 672.93 of the *Criminal Code*. In this case, K.B. Phillips J. set out that the justice presiding at the bail hearing considered the appropriateness of judicial interim release through the lens of section 515 of the *Criminal Code* and also considered whether the accused should be released in the context of section 672.93 of the *Criminal Code*. Justice Phillips found that these "two lenses, so to speak, are distinct from each other."[203] Although the Superior Court has jurisdiction to review the disposition made at the bail hearing under section 515 of the *Criminal Code*, the Superior Court "has no jurisdiction to review a justice's decision under s. 672.93, or indeed any part of Part 20.1 of the *Criminal Code*."[204] An appeal against any disposition made by a court or review board or a placement decision is made to the provincial Court of Appeal.

* * * * *

Notice
(1.1) If the justice releases the accused, notice shall be given to the court or Review Board, as the case may be, that made the disposition or assessment order.

Order of justice pending decision of Review Board
(2) If the justice is satisfied that there are reasonable grounds to believe that the accused has contravened or failed to comply with a disposition or an assessment order, the justice, pending a hearing of a Review Board with respect to the disposition or a hearing of a court or Review Board with respect to the assessment order, may make an order that is appropriate in the circumstances

203 *R. v. Tenegu*, [2020] O.J. No. 4263 at para. 3 (S.C.J.).
204 *Ibid.* at para. 4.

in relation to the accused, including an order that the accused be returned to a place that is specified in the disposition or assessment order. If the justice makes an order under this subsection, notice shall be given to the court or Review Board, as the case may be, that made the disposition or assessment order.

1991, c. 43, s. 4; 2005, c. 22, s. 36

Powers of Review Board

672.94 Where a Review Board receives a notice given under subsection 672.93(1.1) or (2), it may exercise the powers and shall perform the duties mentioned in sections 672.5 and 672.81 to 672.83 as if the Review Board were reviewing a disposition.

1991, c. 43, s. 4; 2005, c. 22, s. 36

Regulations

672.95 The Governor in Council may make regulations

(a) prescribing anything that may be prescribed under this Part; and

(b) generally to carry out the purposes and provisions of this Part.

APPENDIX A

Fitness to Stand Trial and Criminal Responsibility: An Introductory Overview

THE PRESUMPTION OF FITNESS AND RELEVANT DEFINITIONS

Every accused person is presumed to be fit to stand trial until the contrary is proven on a balance of probabilities, pursuant to section 672.22 of the *Criminal Code*:

> **Presumption of fitness**
> **672.22** An accused is presumed fit to stand trial unless the court is satisfied on the balance of probabilities that the accused is unfit to stand trial. [1991, c. 43, s. 4]

The requirement that an accused be "fit to stand trial" stems from the ancient notion that an accused must be present to respond to accusations of the state. That basic requirement developed into a more refined view that the accused must not only be physically present but mentally present as well. Accordingly, rules originally developed at common law were codified in 1992 as part of Bill C-30 and are contained in section 2 of the *Criminal Code*, as set out below:

DEFINITIONS FROM SECTION 2

> **"mental disorder"** means a disease of the mind;
> **"unfit to stand trial"** means unable on account of mental disorder to conduct a defence at any stage of the proceedings before a verdict is rendered or to instruct counsel to do so, and, in particular, unable on account of mental disorder to
> (a) understand the nature or object of the proceedings,
> (b) understand the possible consequences of the proceedings, or
> (c) communicate with counsel

At any stage of the proceedings *before* a verdict is rendered, the court may direct that the issue of the accused's fitness be tried if the court has reasonable grounds to believe that the accused is unfit to stand trial, pursuant to section 672.23(1):

> **Court may direct issue to be tried**
> **672.23** (1) Where the court has reasonable grounds, at any stage of the proceedings before a verdict is rendered, to believe that the accused is unfit to stand trial, the court may direct, of its own motion or on application of the accused or the prosecutor, that the issue of fitness of the accused be tried.

Most often, the fitness issue arises at the accused's first appearance and is resolved prior to arraignment. However, the issue may arise during the course of a trial or preliminary hearing and may arise on multiple occasions. It is therefore not subject to rules regarding *res judicata*.

THE TEST

Over the years there has been much controversy within and among the judiciary, among academics, within the bar, and among the psychiatric forensic experts called to give evidence with respect to the so-called *Taylor* test. *Taylor*, below, has been the source of much debate and confusion over the years; said *inter alia* to be internally inconsistent, said to set the bar too low, said to start off with three fitness criteria (section 2) yet concludes with one singular test.

However, recently, the Ontario Court of Appeal released its decision in *R. v. Bharwani*,[1] which rewrites *Taylor* in a way that comports much more closely with how the various practitioners and stakeholders felt the test should operate. A five-judge panel of the Court of Appeal revisited the substance of the test for "unfit to stand trial."[2]

While the Court in *Bharwani* did not overturn *Taylor*, it has been "explained" in a way that one might say amounts to as much. Gone are the duelling "limited cognitive capacity" and "analytic capacity" tests. Gone is any notion that the accused must be able to act in their own "best interests."[3] Gone is the idea that an accused needn't be rational as they are subjected to prosecution. Gone is any notion that there are three "tests" to consider. We now have one test — "the fitness test."[4]

The starting point in considering unfitness to stand trial is, as set out above, in section 2 of the *Criminal Code*.

This definition is said to be merely a codification of the existing common law. The three "in particulars" are now with *Bharwani* clarified to be "touchstones" along with the other *Taylor* test questions[5] that may be considered in informing the fundamental question as to whether or not an accused is *unable on account of mental disorder to conduct a defence at any stage of the proceedings before a verdict is rendered or to instruct counsel to do so.*

As set out in the excerpts below, to be fit, the accused must be capable of communicating rationally with counsel or the court. The accused must have a reality-based understanding of their legal situation, be able to maintain a meaningful presence, and have the capacity to meaningfully participate in the trial process. These are touchstones for the fitness inquiry and the determination of the fundamental question of whether the accused can fairly participate.

Very importantly, the Court underlines that while there is one singular test — "the fitness test" — it has to be applied in a contextualized manner. So, as has been suggested in the past, two quite different clinical entities may be deemed "fit to stand trial" as a function of their quite different legal predicaments, timelines, degrees of participation required, complexity, etc. Elasticity is an inherent part of the contextualized analysis. A nuanced approach must be taken.

More recently, in July 2025, the Supreme Court of Canda in *R. v. Bharwani*,[6] reviewed and upheld the decision of the Ontario Court of Appeal. The Court concluded that an accused is fit to stand trial when they are able to make and communicate reality-based decisions in the conduct of their defence or instruct counsel to do so:

1 *R v. Bharwani*, 2023 ONCA 203, appeal to the SCC heard October 10, 2024, [2023] S.C.C.A. No. 236.

2 *Ibid.*

3 While it is true, as the Court points out, that we do not second-guess the wisdom of other accused's tactical decisions therefore why should this decision-making autonomy be considered as part of the unfit test, it is arguably problematic if bad decisions are being driven by mental disorder?

4 The test is actually the "unfitness to stand trial test" in that we are all presumed to be "fit," the test pertains to those who may not be (section 2).

5 This has always been a mischaracterization/misnomer. These questions came from an old Law Reform Commission of Canada study report as questions that could be of assistance in informing a decision as to one's unfitness.

6 2025 SCC 256.

> To conclude, the text, statutory context, and purpose of the definition of "unfit to stand trial" support an interpretation of the capacity threshold that requires an accused to be able to make reality-based decisions in the conduct of their defence and intelligibly communicate these decisions to counsel or the court. This necessitates a reality-based understanding of the nature or object of and possible consequences of the proceedings, as well as an ability to understand the available options and their consequences, and to select between those options when making decisions. The accused is not required to make decisions that are in their best interests, but cannot be overwhelmed by delusions, hallucinations, or other symptoms of their mental disorder when making and communicating these decisions [at para. 77, emphases added].

> The primary consideration is always assessing the extent to which an accused's mental disorder impairs their understanding of reality when making decisions in their defence [at para. 78].
> This level of capacity falls short of requiring effective or wise decisions. That an accused may make objectively poor decisions in the conduct of their defence is irrelevant to the issue of their fitness to stand trial [at para. 81, emphasis added].

The Court went on to say that the same standard of fitness applies to all accused, whether represent-ed or not (the Court of Appeal indicated that the absence or presence of counsel may be relevant to that assessment). Borrowing from the Court of Appeal's earlier decision, the ability to conduct a defence in this context encompasses: 1) the right to challenge the Crown's case, 2) the right to advance a de-fence, and 3) the right to address the trier of fact. To be fit, an accused must also be able to receive disclosure and understand the concept of disclosure. And, depending upon the legal context, an accused must not only have the capacity to communicate about ordinary matters; the accused must "comprehend the details of the evidence, which in a case of this nature must constitute a minute investigation" (Pritchard, p. 135).

***Clayton (Re)*, 2025 ONCA 305** – The court or Review Board, in applying the fitness test, must do so "contextually" as set out by the Court of Appeal in *Bharwani*. Specifically, the court or Review Board must consider the accused's specific legal predicament or specific legal context. It may be, for example, that an accused is deemed "fit" in respect one charge but unfit in respect of other more complicated charges that will require more engagement over a longer period of time.

R. v. Bharwani, 2023 ONCA 203 at paras. 107, 110–12, and 167

> [107] To summarize, properly interpreted, *Taylor* stands for the following propositions:
>
> 1. The s. 2 definition of "unfit to stand trial" — which at its core concerns itself with whether the accused is unable on account of mental disorder to conduct a defence or instruct counsel to do so – is the test for determining fitness. While it is open to the court to interpret that test in accordance with the principles of statutory interpretation, it is not open to the court to ignore the statutory test and create a new one.
> 2. As the s. 2 definition is a statutory entrenchment of the prior case law in the area, that case law guides the interpretation of its content. Based on that case law, an accused must be capable of communicating "rationally" with counsel or the court in order to be fit. This includes an inquiry into whether an accused is able to understand relevant information, apply that information in the context of their decision-making, and intelligibly communicate.
> 3. The touchstones of the s. 2 fitness inquiry — whether the accused can be meaningfully present and meaningfully participate at their trial — inform a purposive interpretation and application of the s. 2 fitness test. They do not constitute a stand-alone test for fitness.

4. The accused need not have the capacity to engage in analytic thinking in the sense that the accused need not be capable of making decisions in their own best interests.[7]

. . .

[110] Some have suggested that the fitness test from *Taylor* can simply be applied by obtaining answers to the *Taylor* test questions.

[111] Let us pause here to observe that the label "*Taylor* test questions" is a bit of a mystery. The questions, as previously set out in these reasons, are of uncertain origin. However, one thing is for certain: they are not to be found in the *Taylor* decision.

[112] In any event, for the reasons previously given, we agree with all counsel on appeal that those questions should never be used as the definitive test for fitness. While the questions are undoubtedly helpful in providing insight into an accused's fitness, they will often fall short of the mark in terms of exploring whether an accused is unfit to stand trial because unfitness, as a state and as a legal standard, is far more complex. Quite simply, as already shown, determining an accused's fitness to stand trial demands a much more nuanced inquiry than simply placing tick marks beside seven questions that can be answered "correctly".

. . .

[167] To sum up, the following principles should inform all fitness assessments:

1. There is one fitness test for all accused, whether represented by counsel or not. This test is applied contextually.
2. The test for fitness is set out in the statutory definition of "unfit to stand trial" in s. 2 of the *Criminal Code.*
3. A person is unfit to stand trial if, on account of mental disorder, the person is unable to conduct a defence or to instruct counsel to do so.
4. The purpose of the s. 2 fitness test is to ensure that the accused can be meaningfully present and meaningfully participate at their trial. These touchstones inform a purposive interpretation and application of the s. 2 fitness test and do not themselves constitute a stand-alone test.
5. The *Taylor* test questions are not a sufficient surrogate for assessing fitness but are helpful in providing insights into an accused's abilities in relation to the s. 2 criteria. Applying the fitness test is more nuanced than the questions recognize.
6. The accused must have a reality-based understanding of the nature and object and possible consequences of the proceedings.
7. The accused must have the ability to make decisions. This involves the ability to understand available options, the ability to select from those options, the ability to understand the basic consequences arising from those options, and the ability to intelligibly communicate to either counsel or the court the decision arrived upon.
8. The accused need not have the capacity to engage in analytic thinking in the sense that the accused need not be capable of making decisions in their own best interests.

Note: While the court in *Bharwani* did not overturn *Taylor*, it nevertheless "explained" it in a way that renders much of the *Taylor* language obsolete and no longer applicable. Therefore, cases that have relied upon or incorporated *Taylor* must now be read through a *Bharwani* lens.

7 While it is true that what is in "one's own best interests" is a matter of perspective, one might argue that where an objective failure to act in one's own best interests is the product of a mental disorder that has rendered the accused incapable of rational thought, the "rules" should step in to protect.

The case of ***R. v. Taylor*, [1992] O.J. No. 2394 (C.A.)** sets out that the test for fitness to stand trial is the "limited cognitive capacity test":

> The test to be applied is one of limited cognitive ability, whether the accused understands the nature and object of the proceedings, understands the possible consequences, and can recount to counsel the necessary facts relating to the offence in such a way that counsel can then properly present a defence. It is not necessary that the accused be able to meet some higher test of analytic capacity or capacity to make rational decisions beneficial to himself.

This test requires that the accused have only a rudimentary factual understanding of their legal predicament. A "rational" understanding is not required, nor is it necessary that the accused be able to act in their own best interests.[8] From ***R. v. Steele* (1991), 63 C.C.C. (3d) 149 (Que. C.A.)**:

> An accused is incapable of conducting his defence if he cannot distinguish between available pleas; does not understand the nature or purpose of the proceedings, including the respective roles of the judge, jury and counsel; is unable to communicate with counsel rationally or make critical decisions on counsel's advice; or is unable to take the stand to testify if necessary.

The *Taylor* test was adopted by the Supreme Court of Canada in ***R. v. Whittle*, [1994] 2 S.C.R. 914.** In that case, the schizophrenic accused was arrested for failure to pay fines. While in custody, he expressed a desire to speak to police about a murder and three robberies. Appropriate rights to counsel were provided by attending officers. The accused waived his right to silence and wanted to speak to police about the crimes to stop the voices in his head. The Supreme Court of Canada found that the statements were voluntary and admissible. The accused understood what he was saying, he understood the court process, and was fit to instruct counsel. As a result of the voices telling the accused to unburden himself, he simply did not care about the consequences. The Supreme Court of Canada confirmed that the accused does not need to act in his own best interests.

The *Taylor* test was also confirmed in ***R. v. Morrissey*, 2007 ONCA 770, leave to appeal refused [2008] S.C.C.A. No. 102.**

The judge is the ultimate decision-maker with respect to fitness. A psychiatrist's opinion that the accused is not fit is not determinative.

"REASONABLE GROUNDS" FOR A JUDGE TO ORDER A FITNESS ASSESSMENT

What amounts to "reasonable grounds" for a judge to order a fitness assessment (section 672.11(a)) and then direct a trial of that issue (section 672.23(1)1)? There is no specific formula to answer that question. From arrest to the courtroom, the accused's behaviour, words, or appearance may be used to reasonably infer whether they have the capacity to understand the constituent elements of the process. Psychotic symptoms or behaviour invariably qualify, but even a psychotic accused may be fit, provided the subject matter of the delusions or hallucinations neither impinges on their understanding of the legal predicament and the process, nor interferes with their participation in it. The table below provides some guidelines of "appropriate" and "inappropriate" reasons for a judge to order a fitness assessment. Fairness — the value upon which the process rests — dictates that any uncertainty weigh in the favour of the accused.

8 For a critique of the *Taylor* decision, see R.D. Schneider & H. Bloom, "*R. v. Taylor*: A Decision Not in the Best Interests of Some Mentally Ill Accused" (1995) 38 *Crim. L.Q.* 183.

Reasons For a Judge to Order a Fitness Assessment*

Appropriate Reasons	Inappropriate Reasons
• Specific information seen or heard that the accused does not understand and/or cannot participate in court process. • Evidence of hallucinations and delusions affecting the accused's comprehension of the proceedings and/or ability to participate in them. • Evidence of significant disordered thought — confusion. • Evidence of difficulty processing information. • Inability to concentrate. • Apathy/Withdrawal. • Muteness. • Marked disruptive behaviour together with evidence of abnormal affect/perception/thought processes/delusions. • Information or evidence of marked impairment of mood (significant depression or elation). • The patient is suicidal.	• The accused has a psychiatric history (with no clear evidence of active mental illness). • The accused or counsel asks that the accused go to hospital. • The accused is homeless. • To understand how and why the accused became a habitual criminal. • To provide treatment for an otherwise non-compliant accused under the guise of a need to assess them. • The accused is angry and loud (with no evidence/history of mental disorder). • The accused's family conveys that the accused should be in hospital and not jail. • The accused is unkempt, disheveled, or malodorous. • The allegations are bizarre or disclose that the accused's behaviour at the relevant time was bizarre (absent other information bearing on the issue of the accused's fitness). • The accused interrupts the proceedings (with no evidence/history of mental disorder). • The accused is seen muttering to themself.

* Note that the above represent guidelines. Evidence of a number of items listed under the "Inappropriate Reasons" column, taken together, may reasonably raise a question.

FLUCTUATING FITNESS

Fitness fluctuates, particularly if the mentally ill individual is psychotic. Section 2 requires that the accused be capable of "conduct[ing] a defence." It is a reasonable interpretation that fitness to stand trial has a future connotation or element of prospectivity since the actual trial will be occurring days or weeks in the future. If it cannot be predicted that the accused will maintain fitness to stand trial for the foreseeable future so as to endure and participate in a trial of some complexity, then the accused cannot be said to be fit to stand trial, even if the examiner catches them during a "fit interval." An accused who intends to plead guilty and who will be sentenced in short order probably requires a narrower window of predictable fitness to stand trial.[9]

WHAT IF THE FITNESS ISSUE ARISES AFTER A VERDICT IS PRONOUNCED?

Where the fitness issue arises *after a verdict* is pronounced and *prior to sentencing* or *during* the course of sentencing, the Part XX.1 *Criminal Code* statutory provisions do not apply. It may be that, from a common law or *Charter of Rights* perspective, the prosecution may not be able to proceed. This issue — and the problem created by the definition in section 2 — is in need of parliamentary review and would benefit from amendments that would cure this rare but difficult situation.[10]

9 For a fuller consideration of the fitness to stand trial issue, see R.D. Schneider & H. Bloom, *Fitness to Stand Trial: Fairness First & Foremost* (Toronto: Irwin Law, 2018).

10 For a fuller discussion of this problem, see R.D. Schneider, "Fitness to be Sentenced" (1998) 41 *C.L.Q.* 261.

A summary of the relevant caselaw on this point is below, including *R. v. B. (G.)* and *R. v. Morrison*, where the remedy imposed was to "read in" additional words to bridge the gap in the legislation:

***R. v. Morrison*, 2016 SKQB 259** — The applicant faced a dangerous offender application after being convicted of break and enter and sexual assault causing bodily harm. The defence ordered a fitness assessment, which concluded that the accused was not fit. The court granted the "reading-in remedy" sought by defence counsel, allowing for the fitness hearing to occur post-verdict as the language of the impugned provisions violated the accused's section 7 *Charter* rights and were not justified under section 1 of the *Charter.* The court found it was necessary that the accused be able to instruct counsel during the dangerous offender sentencing hearing.

***R. v. Jaser*, 2015 ONSC 4729** — This case involved two co-accused, Jaser and Esseghaier. After a jury trial, convictions were entered for both accused for offences of conspiracy to derail a passenger train for the benefit of a terrorist group and conspiracy to commit murder for the benefit of a terrorist group. During the sentencing hearing, the issue arose as to whether the court should inquire into Esseghaier's fitness by ordering a psychiatric assessment. Esseghaier consented to a psychiatric assessment under section 21 of the Ontario *Mental Health Act* as there was no provision in the *Criminal Code* providing for a psychiatric assessment pending sentence. The court found that section 7 of the *Charter* requires that a trial judge possess the power to inquire into the "limited cognitive capacity" or "operating mind" of the accused at a sentencing hearing but that extending sections 2 and 672.23(1) by a "reading in" remedy in *R. v. B. (G.)* was not appropriate as it would give rise to significant criminal law policy questions and would require amendments to sections 672.38 and 672.47 of the *Criminal Code* to expand the jurisdiction of the Review Board. The court made a further section 21 assessment order to address the issue of Esseghaier's fitness at a sentencing hearing.

***R. v. B. (G.)*, [2003] O.J. No. 784 (S.C.J.)**[11] — The Crown brought a dangerous offender application after the accused was convicted of several charges of assault, sexual assault, unlawful confinement, and criminal harassment against his girlfriend. Following the verdict but before sentencing, the accused became unfit to communicate with counsel, who brought an application arguing that sections 2 and 672.23(1) of the *Criminal Code* violated section 7 of the *Charter* since it addressed only the issue to stand trial and did not provide for unfitness during sentencing. The application was granted, and the court found that the "legislative gap" violated the accused's section 7 *Charter* right. The accused's ability to participate in the dangerous offender application was essential. The infringement was not justified under section 1 of the *Charter.* At para. 48, the remedy ordered was to "read-in" the words "at any stage of the proceedings before a verdict is rendered or sentence imposed."

THE FITNESS ASSESSMENT IN PRACTICE: A "HOW-TO" OVERVIEW

The analysis begins with the presumption in section 672.22 of the *Criminal Code* that the accused is fit to stand trial unless the court is otherwise satisfied on a balance of probabilities.

According to section 2 of the *Criminal Code*, an accused is unfit to stand trial if they are unable on account of mental disorder to conduct a defence at any stage of the proceedings before a verdict is rendered or to instruct counsel to do so, and, in particular, unable on account of mental disorder to:

1) understand the *nature* or *object* of the proceedings
2) understand the possible *consequences* of the proceedings or
3) *communicate* and instruct counsel

---

11 This case is also referred to as *R. v. Balliram* in the caselaw.

The below chart sets out the basic questions and answers that all counsel should be familiar with when faced with the fitness issue.

Question	Answer	Section
Who can raise the fitness issue?	The court on its own motion or on application of the accused or prosecutor.	672.23(1)
Who has the burden of showing the accused is unfit?	The party bringing the application.	672.23(2)
What standard must be met to hold a fitness hearing?	A fitness hearing can only be held by the court if there are *reasonable grounds* to believe that fitness is an issue.	672.23(1)
How can reasonable grounds be shown?	Expert evidence is not needed. Questions should be asked of the accused that relate to the nature or object of the proceedings and its consequences. Questions can be asked to determine the accused's ability to communicate with or instruct counsel; counsel may also speak to this issue. Traditionally, the criteria set out in section 2 have been explored through a set of questions such as the following: • What are the roles of the various people in the courtroom? • What are the charges the accused is facing? • What are the available pleas? • What are the consequences of a conviction? • What is the meaning of an oath? • What is perjury?	
What if there are reasonable grounds to believe fitness is an issue?	An assessment order ("Form 48 assessment") should be requested. A court may order an assessment of the mental condition of the accused if it has reasonable grounds to believe that such evidence is necessary to determine whether the accused is unfit.	672.11(a)
How long can an assessment order be in place?	In general, an assessment order shall not be in force for more than thirty days. There is an exception in fitness cases, that the order shall not be for greater than five days except on consent of the accused. If consent is provided, the order shall be for no more than thirty days. In compelling circumstances, there is an exception that allows the order to remain in place for sixty days.	672.14(1) 672.14(2) 672.14(3)
What if the doctor provides an opinion that the accused is unfit in the Form 48 assessment?	The court will hold a fitness hearing and it will be on the party that raised the issue of fitness to prove on a balance of probabilities that the accused is unfit. Evidence will be called by either filing the doctor's report on consent or having the doctor testify. The test to be applied at the fitness hearing is the "limited cognitive capacity test," described above.	2
When in proceedings can a fitness hearing be held?	At any stage of proceedings before a verdict is rendered. Caselaw has permitted a fitness hearing to occur after the verdict but before sentencing.	2; 672.23(1)
Who tries the fitness issue?	The trier of fact, either a judge alone (s. 672.27) or a jury (s. 672.28).	672.27; 672.28
What are the available verdicts on the fitness issue?	There are only two verdicts with respect to the issue of fitness: (1) fit; and (2) unfit. If the accused is found fit, then proceedings continue as usual (s. 672.28).	672.28

PROCEDURE IN A FITNESS HEARING

Calling the doctor who provided the opinion in the Form 48 assessment is a possibility, but not a necessity. If the doctor is called, then the doctor must be qualified as an expert in their field to provide opinion evidence. The relevant field is typically forensic psychiatry. If the other party does not consent to the proposed expert's qualification, then the expert admissibility *voir dire* occurs in the normal course.

To be admitted as an expert witness, the following *Mohan* criteria must be met: (1) relevance; (2) necessity in assisting the trier of fact; (3) the absence of any exclusionary rule; and (4) a properly qualified expert. A further cost benefit analysis will be completed at the judicial gatekeeping stage.[12]

The doctor's report should typically be filed as an exhibit during the proceedings. The doctor is typically permitted to rely on the report as a reference throughout testimony. In going through the report in court, the doctor will provide evidence with respect to the accused's response to various questions, including those related to the roles of the parties in the criminal justice system (judge, Crown, and defence), the nature of the charges, the possible outcomes of the criminal proceedings, and the accused's understanding of an oath and the importance to tell the truth. Cross-examination will proceed in the usual course.

If the defence raised the issue of fitness, the defence may call the accused after the court hears the testimony of the doctor; this will inevitably depend upon the evidence of the expert. When cross-examining the accused, the same issues addressed by the doctor should be put to the accused. Non-legal, simple terms should be used when cross-examining the accused. The accused, however, is not a compellable witness.

Lastly, submissions are made as to whether the accused is unfit to stand trial. The below chart provides the questions and answers that arise when the accused is found unfit after the assessment order is completed:

Question	Answer	Section
What if the accused is found unfit after an assessment order is completed?	If a treatment order would assist the person, then only the Crown can ask for a treatment order.	672.58
	On application of the Crown, the court may order that the accused be treated for a period not exceeding 60 days.	672.58
	Neither the judge nor defence counsel can make an application for a treatment order.	672.45, 672.47
	If the Crown does not apply for a treatment order, options available to defence counsel are: (1) request a disposition hearing before the court, or (2) have the matter traversed to the Review Board.	
Does the Crown need to provide notice of its intention to seek a treatment order?	Yes. The Crown must provide written notice to the accused. Notice must be provided as soon as practicable.	672.6(1)
What evidence must the court hear to issue a treatment order?	The court can only make a treatment order under s. 672.58 when it is satisfied on the basis of the testimony of a medical practitioner, that a specific treatment should be administered to the accused for the purpose of making the accused fit to stand trial.	
	As a result, the medical practitioner needs to be qualified as an expert to provide opinion evidence. Upon qualification, the medical practitioner will be able to provide testimony.	

12 *R. v. Mohan*, [1994] 2 S.C.R. 9 at 20–21.

Question	Answer	Section
	The testimony of the medical practitioner shall include a statement that the medical practitioner has made an assessment of the accused and is of the opinion, based on the grounds specified, that (a) the accused, at the time of the assessment, was unfit to stand trial; (b) the psychiatric treatment and any other related medical treatment specified by the medical practitioner will likely make the accused fit to stand trial within a period not exceeding sixty days and that without that treatment the accused is likely to remain unfit to stand trial; (c) the risk of harm to the accused from the psychiatric and other related medical treatment specified is not disproportionate to the benefit anticipated to be derived from it; and (d) the psychiatric and other related medical treatment specified is the least restrictive and least intrusive treatment that could, in the circumstances, be specified for the purpose referred to in subsection (1), considering the opinions referred to in paragraphs (b) and (c). Note that cross-examination of the medical practitioner is permitted. Once all evidence is heard, both parties can make submissions for the court to consider in arriving at a decision.	672.59
Does the hospital need to consent to the treatment order?	Yes. The court can only make a treatment order with the consent of the hospital. In compelling circumstances, the court may make the order without the hospital's consent (see ***R. v. Conception*, [2014] 3 SCR 82**). For that reason, it would be wise for Crown counsel to determine the availability of a bed for an accused before embarking upon an application for a treatment order. An application may be denied where the wait times are unreasonable.	672.62
What if the treatment order is granted?	A treatment order can be granted for up to sixty days, with the limitation that if the accused becomes fit before that sixty-day time limit, the accused will be brought back to court.	672.58

Most treatment orders do result in the accused being rendered "fit" within sixty days. Upon the accused's return to court, the issue will be retried where the opinion is that the accused is now fit. Once again, fitness must now be demonstrated on a balance of probabilities.

The below chart provides the questions and answers that arise when the accused is returned to court after the completion of a treatment order, where the opinion of the medical practitioner is that the accused is now fit:

Question	Answer	Section
What procedure occurs if the opinion is that the accused is now fit?	A hearing will be held to determine whether the accused remains unfit to stand trial.	672.32(1)

Question	Answer	Section
Who bears the burden of proof during the hearing?	The burden is on the party that seeks to establish the change to the accused's status of fitness. Note that another assessment order (Form 48) does not need to be done. The medical practitioner's report will be filed, typically on consent and without the medical practitioner actually testifying. There is, however, a right to cross-examine the medical practitioner. The accused may or may not be called by counsel to answer fitness questions but is not compellable. The court will then determine whether the accused remains unfit. If the accused is found fit, they will return to normal court procedures.	672.32(2)
If the accused is found fit, is there a way to *keep* the accused fit?	Yes. If the accused is detained in custody pending trial and is found fit, then the court may order the accused to be detained in a hospital until the trial is completed, if the court has reasonable grounds to believe that the accused would become unfit to stand trial if released. Note that this type of order is colloquially referred to as a "keep fit" order.	672.29

If an unfit accused person becomes fit after a treatment order and the matter results in a conviction, then the issue of pre-sentence credit will arise at the sentencing hearing. An accused person's mental health during their committal period is a relevant consideration for the Court to consider when assessing whether delay caused by the accused person is wrongful. If the accused's conduct that causes a delay in proceedings is "a consequence, entirely or to a significant degree, of his mental and cognitive state",[13] then this conduct would not be considered wrongful in the sentencing context and would not disqualify the accused person from enhanced credit.[14]

It is, however, possible that the accused may remain unfit even after the completion of a treatment order. The below chart provides the questions and answers that arise when the accused remains unfit even after the treatment order is completed:

Question	Answer	Section
What options exist if the accused remains unfit after the completion of a treatment order?	The court may hold a disposition hearing under s. 672.45(1) or the matter could be sent to the Ontario Review Board under s. 672.47.	672.45(1); 672.47
What happens if the court holds a disposition hearing?	At the disposition hearing, the court shall make a disposition in respect of the accused, if it is satisfied that it can readily do so and that a disposition should be made without delay. Note that even if the court makes a disposition (other than an absolute discharge), the matter will ultimately go to the Review Board for a review of the disposition within ninety days, pursuant to s. 672.47(3). The court cannot discharge the accused absolutely if the accused is unfit.	672.45(2) 672.47(3)
What happens if the accused is found unfit and no disposition has been made by the court?	The Review Board shall, as soon as practicable but not later than forty-five days after the verdict was rendered, hold a hearing and make a disposition.	672.47(1)

13 *R. v. J.W.*, 2025 SCC 16 at para. 107.

14 *Ibid.* at paras. 106–109.

Question	Answer	Section
What happens to the accused while awaiting to be before the Review Board?	The *status quo* continues pending the Review Board hearing. If the accused is in custody, for example, they will remain in custody. If the accused is on a release order with conditions, for example, the accused will continue to be on that same release order. However, on cause being shown, the accused may be ordered to hospital pending appearance in court.	672.46 672.46(2)
What happens to the prosecution if the unfit accused goes to the Review Board?	In adult matters, the Crown must prove a *prima facie* case every two years. The prosecution can be continued if the accused one day becomes fit. If the accused is a young person, the Crown must prove a *prima facie* case every year. Note that if a *prima facie* case is not made, the court shall acquit the accused.	672.33(1) *YCJA* 141(10) 672.33(6)

NOT CRIMINALLY RESPONSIBLE: AN INTRODUCTORY OVERVIEW

INTRODUCTION: THE PRESUMPTION AND DEFINITIONS

In 1992, with Bill C-30, Parliament replaced the "Insanity Defence" with the defence of "Not Criminally Responsible on Account of Mental Disorder" ("NCR" or "NCRMD"). The statutory changes consist largely of a modernization of the language employed. Section 16 of the *Criminal Code* of Canada articulates the general principle that no person who committed an offence while suffering from a mental disorder that rendered the person incapable of appreciating the nature and quality of the act or omission or of knowing that it was wrong may be convicted. It should be emphasized at the outset that the test is strictly legal, not medical.

Everyone is presumed to be criminally responsible until the contrary is proven on a balance of probabilities. Mental disorder is a necessary but not sufficient condition required for a finding of being not criminally responsible. The defence of mental disorder is set out in section 16(1) of the *Criminal Code*:

> **Defence of Mental Disorder**
> **16** (1) No person is criminally responsible for an act committed or an omission made while suffering from a mental disorder that rendered the person incapable of appreciating the nature and quality of the act or omission or of knowing that it was wrong.
>
> (2) Every person is presumed not to suffer from a mental disorder so as to be exempt from criminal responsibility by virtue of subsection (1), until the contrary is proved on the balance of probabilities.
>
> (3) The burden of proof that an accused was suffering from a mental disorder so as to be exempt from criminal responsibility is on the party that raises the issue.

R.S., 1985, c. C-46, s. 16; R.S., 1985, c. 27 (1st Supp.), s. 185(F); 1991, c. 43, s. 2

Upon a verdict that the accused was NCR at the relevant time, the provisions of Part XX.1 of the *Criminal Code* apply. The accused may be detained in hospital, discharged subject to conditions, or, if not a significant threat to the safety of the public, discharged absolutely. While the court may issue a disposition upon the verdict, the matter is typically referred to the provincial or territorial Review Board.

DOES THE ACCUSED WANT TO RAISE THE "DEFENCE"?

A very important question for counsel to ask their experts (especially when retained privately) is, "Do I want to raise the NCR defence?" The answer to this question will require careful questioning of the expert and discussion with the client. Upon a verdict of NCR, the accused will have a disposition hearing and a disposition will be rendered, either by the court at first instance or later by the Review Board.

Given that the objective of most accused is the fastest path to liberty, the raising of an NCR defence may be counterproductive. Counsel must inquire of the expert — hopefully an expert in forensic psychiatry with intimate knowledge of the Review Board system — two key questions: (1) upon a verdict of NCR, will the accused be found a "significant threat to the safety of the public"?; and (2) if found to be a significant threat to the safety of the public, what is the most probable "necessary and appropriate disposition"? If the opinion of the expert is that it cannot be shown that the accused is a significant threat to the safety of the public, the accused may look forward to an absolute discharge. The matter will then be terminated with no further obligation to the Review Board or the courts. If, on the other hand, the accused is likely going to be found a significant threat to the safety of the public, there is a wide variety of possible outcomes. These range from detention in a maximum secure hospital to being discharged from hospital and living in the community with minor encumbrances upon the accused's liberty.

Knowing the likely post-NCR verdict outcome is critical information for counsel to discuss with the accused prior to the receiving of instructions. While the expert cannot make guarantees, counsel will be able to determine with a high degree of certainty what the post-verdict outcome will be. There is no predictable correlation between the seriousness of the offence and the necessary and appropriate disposition. This is logically appropriate. An accused charged with a very minor offence may, upon assessment, be viewed as a very dangerous person. On the other hand, an accused charged with a very serious offence may be viewed as not a significant threat.

The same tactic must be employed by Crown counsel prior to deciding whether or not to raise the "defence." If the opinion is that the accused is not a "significant threat to the safety of the public," yet the Crown wishes to have long-term supervision, they may be better off letting a conviction register and then seeking a long period of probation.

WHEN MAY THE ISSUE ARISE?

As with any defence, the accused may assert this defence at the outset of the trial or may raise it at the conclusion of the Crown's case if, and only if, there is a case to meet calling for a defence. This may be done as late as upon a finding of guilt but prior to conviction.

As a result of the Supreme Court of Canada's decision in ***R. v. Swain*, [1991] 1 S.C.R. 933**, a new common law rule was established that the Crown may also raise the "defence" over the accused's objection at one of two junctures. First, the Crown may raise the issue of criminal responsibility when, during the accused's own defence, the accused puts their mental capacity for intent in issue. Second, the Crown may raise the issue after the trier of fact has concluded that the accused is otherwise guilty.

Procedurally, raising this issue allows for a "bifurcated trial." If the issue is not raised by the accused at the outset of the trial, the issue may be raised by either party, but only after the accused is proven to be guilty. The accused may call evidence at the first phase of the bifurcated trial and may raise other issues or defences such as identification or alibi, while reserving the right to respond with the defence of NCR only if the trier of fact finds the accused guilty.

CRITICAL APPRAISAL OF AN EXPERT'S CRIMINAL RESPONSIBILITY REPORT

A non-exhaustive list of the errors experts make in evaluating accused with respect to criminal responsibility includes the following:

- failing to understand the legal standard for absent criminal responsibility
- assuming that mental disorder is synonymous with lack of criminal responsibility
- failing to hypothesize and deal with the prospect the accused is malingering
- relying on inadequate information
- failing to address the accused's mental state with respect to each and every offence with which they are charged

The error with respect to the last point is the expert incorrectly assuming that the same mental state was operative so as to exempt the accused from responsibility with respect to each and every charge. The requisite mental element for an array of charges may, of course, be different.

A report that fails to acknowledge alternative interpretations of the facts is likely going to present problems in that there will inevitably be more than one way to "connect the dots." Counsel must communicate that they need to hear "the good, the bad, and the ugly" with respect to their client and the probability of a successful defence. Receiving a favourable report is not going to be helpful when, at trial, counsel is blind-sided with cross-examination of their expert that had not been anticipated. Counsel must be alerted to the frailties of the case and why, among the competing theories, the formulation of their expert is the most parsimonious and compelling. And, as mentioned above, while the first question of the expert is, "Do I have an NCR defence?" the second and equally important question is, "Do I want an NCR defence?" Knowing the most likely disposition is of critical importance. For these reasons, counsel will often ask their expert for an opinion orally prior to having a report prepared. It may be that no report will be sought given this preliminary communication between counsel and expert.

THE NCR PROCEDURE IN PRACTICE: A "HOW-TO" OVERVIEW

The analysis begins with the presumption in section 16(2) of the *Criminal Code* that the accused does not suffer from a mental disorder so as to be exempt from criminal responsibility.

The below chart sets out the basic questions and answers that all counsel should be familiar with when faced with the NCR issue:

Question	Answer	Section
Who can raise the NCR issue?	The Crown or defence counsel can raise the NCR issue. The court should not enter the fray with respect to an NCR "defence" (see ***R. v. Piette*, 2005 BCSC 1724**).	16(3)
Who bears the burden of proof in raising the NCR issue?	The burden of proof that an accused was suffering from mental disorder to exempt them from criminal responsibility is on the party that raises the issue.	16(3)
What standard must be met to order an assessment of criminal responsibility?	Reasonable grounds. A court may order an assessment ("Form 48") of the mental condition of the accused if it has reasonable grounds to believe that such evidence is necessary to determine whether the accused was, at the time of the commission of the alleged offence, suffering from a mental disorder so as to be exempt from criminal responsibility.	672.11(b)

Question	Answer	Section
How can reasonable grounds be shown to support the issuance of an assessment order?	Expert evidence is not required in order to meet this threshold (only reasonable grounds), which *may* include medical evidence. The reasonable grounds requirement is typically satisfied with the submissions of counsel. The accused may seek an assessment order at any point in the proceedings whereas the Crown has only two portals: (1) where the accused puts their mental state in issue, or (2) where the Crown can demonstrate reasonable grounds to believe the accused may not be criminally responsible.	672.12
How long can the assessment order remain in place?	An assessment order shall not be in force for more than thirty days.	672.14(1)

PROCEDURE IN AN NCR ASSESSMENT ORDER HEARING

Either party may make an application to the court for an assessment order under section 672.11 for the purpose of determining criminal responsibility. For tactical reasons, defence counsel may opt to avoid the court-ordered assessment (which will result in a report returning to the presiding judge and being distributed to Crown counsel) and instead retain an expert privately. Often, accused will be without funds for such a disbursement, necessitating applications to Legal Aid for the purpose of retaining experts. Most forensic psychiatrists will agree to do a certain percentage of their work at the Legal Aid tariff.

The below chart provides some of the questions and answers that arise when the accused is found NCR after the assessment order is completed:

Question	Answer	Section
What happens if an NCR verdict is obtained?	The accused then falls under the jurisdiction of the Review Board, which shall consist of not fewer than five members appointed by the lieutenant governor in council of the province.	672.38(1)
When are disposition hearings held after the NCR verdict is found?	Disposition hearings are held within forty-five days of an NCRMD verdict.	672.47
When can disposition review hearings be held?	Disposition review hearings are held no more than twelve months after the most recent disposition review hearing.	672.81
How is an NCR finding considered when reviewing the accused's criminal record?	A verdict of NCR is not a previous conviction. Greater punishments may not be sought on the basis of NCR verdicts.	672.36

APPENDIX B

ORB Rules of Procedure

Schedule A
Review Board
Rules of Procedure

General Principle

1. These Rules shall be liberally construed to secure the just, most expeditious and least expensive determination of every matter before the Review Board.
2. Definitions

   "adjournment" refers to a situation where the presiding Chairperson orders that a hearing is to continue on another date.

   "annual hearing" refers to a review of an accused's Disposition as set out in s. 672.81 of the *Criminal Code.*

   "hearing" includes "initial hearings", "annual hearings", and any other hearing held pursuant to the provisions of Part XX.1 of the *Criminal Code of Canada*.

   "hospital" refers, in addition to the definition of "hospital" in section 672.1 of the *Criminal Code*, to a single designated facility in which the accused is detained or to which the accused is required to report from time to time as a term in a Disposition.

   "initial hearing" refers to an accused's first hearing before the Review Board.

   "Registrar" refers to the individual, appointed by the Chairperson, who is responsible for the production and distribution of all Dispositions and Reasons.

   "re-schedule" refers to the process of, on the consent of all parties and with the Chairperson's approval, setting a new date for a hearing without the necessity of an application being made to a quorum of the Review Board.

Matters Not Provided for in these Rules

3. Where any matter of procedure is not provided for by these Rules, the Chairperson of the Review Board or the presiding Alternate Chairperson shall determine the procedure to be followed.

Practice Directions

4. A practice direction, notice or guide for proceedings before the Review Board shall be signed by the Chairperson of the Review Board and published in the Ontario Reports.

Effect of Non-Compliance

5. A failure to comply with these Rules is an irregularity and does not render a hearing, or a step, document or order in a hearing a nullity, or the Review Board,
   (1) may grant all necessary amendments or other relief, on such terms as are just, to secure the just determination of the real matters in dispute; and
   (2) only where and as necessary in the interests of justice, may set aside the proceeding or a step, document or order in the proceeding in whole or in part.

Language

6. All procedures are to be in French and/or English.
   6.1 Subject to this Rule, evidence or submissions may be presented in English and/or French.
   6.2 The Board may conduct a hearing or a part of it in French where a request is made:
      (a) by the accused;
      (b) by any other party; or
      (c) by a person seeking party status at the time the application for party status is made.
   6.3 Where a hearing or a part of it is to be conducted in French, the Notice of Hearing shall specify in English and French that the hearing is to be so conducted.
   6.4 Where a written submission or written evidence is provided in either English or French, the Review Board may order any person presenting such written submission or written evidence to provide it in the other language if the Review Board considers it necessary for the fair disposition of the matter.
   6.5 A party requesting that a hearing be conducted in French shall notify the Review Board within seven days of the issuance of the Notice of Hearing.

Time

7. In the computation of time under these Rules or an order, except where a contrary intention appears,
      (1) where there is a reference to a number of days between two events, they shall be counted by excluding the day on which the first event happens and including the day on which the second event happens, even if they are described as clear days or the words "at least" are used;
      (2) where a period of less than seven days is prescribed, statutory holidays shall not be counted;
      (3) where the time for doing an act under these Rules expires on a holiday, the act may be done on the next day that is not a holiday; and
      (4) service of a document, other than an originating process, made after 4 p.m. or at any time on a holiday shall be deemed to have been made on the next day that is not a holiday.
   7.1 Where a time of day is mentioned in these Rules or in any document in a proceeding, the time referred to shall be taken as the time observed locally.
   7.2 The Chairperson of the Review Board or the presiding Alternate Chairperson may by order extend or abridge any time prescribed by these rules or an order, on such terms as are just.
   7.3 A motion for an order extending time may be made before or after the expiration of the time prescribed.

Motions

8. Any matter which arises either prior to or at a hearing which requires a decision or order of the Review Board, other than a Disposition, shall be brought before the Review Board by Notice of Motion.

8.1 A Notice of Motion shall be in writing and shall
   (a) contain the decision or order sought, the grounds upon which the motion is made, and an indication of any oral or other evidence sought to be presented;
   (b) be accompanied by an affidavit setting out a clear and concise statement of the relevant facts, and the documents which will be relied upon and may be made exhibits;
   (c) be accompanied by any other relevant documents that may support the motion; and
   (d) indicate that the date for the hearing of the motion will be fixed by the Review Board.

8.2 The party bringing the motion shall file a copy of the Notice of Motion with the Review Board and serve it on all other parties to the proceeding.

8.3 If the Review Board decides that the motion will be heard, the Review Board shall issue a Notice of Hearing of Motion to all other parties to the hearing at least five days before the motion is scheduled to be heard.

8.4 A person who wishes to respond to the Notice of Motion, or to reply to a response, may file and serve, at any time before the motion is scheduled to be heard, a written response or reply, an indication of any oral evidence sought to be presented, and any document which may support the response or reply.

8.5 The Review Board, in hearing a motion, may permit oral or other evidence in addition to the supporting documents accompanying the notice, response or reply.

8.6 Despite this Rule, a Notice of Motion may be given orally at a hearing and shall be disposed of in accordance with such procedures as the Chairperson or Alternate Chairperson may order.

Response to Notice

9. Where a party, other than the accused, receives Notice of Hearing or motion and does not intend to attend, that party shall give the Review Board written notice not less than three days prior to the date on which that hearing was scheduled or return date of hearing.

Time and Place of Hearing

10. The Chairperson of the Review Board shall determine the date, time and place of all hearings and/or motions.

Constitutional Issues

11. Where the constitutional validity or constitutional applicability of a provision of the *Criminal Code* is being challenged by a party, that party shall provide notice of this intention to all parties, the Attorney General of Canada, the Attorney General of Ontario, and the Review Board no less than fifteen working days before an "annual" hearing and without delay before any "other" hearing. The notice shall state concisely the section which is said to be unconstitutional or *ultra vires*, a brief statement of the argument to be made, and the citation of any cases which are relied upon for support of the argument.

12. Where the constitutional rights and freedoms of an accused are alleged by any party to have been violated and a remedy is being sought, that party shall provide notice of its intention to make such argument to all parties and the Review Board no less than 15 working days before an "annual" hearing and without delay before any "other" hearing. The notice shall state concisely the nature of the alleged violation and remedy sought, a brief statement of the argument to be made, and the citation of any cases which are relied upon for support of the argument.

Transfer Requests from One Hospital to Another

13. In any hearing at which it will be submitted by any party that the accused should be transferred to another hospital, either to which the accused is to report to or be detained at, that party shall provide notice of its intention to all parties as well as the person in charge of the prospective receiving hospital no less than four weeks prior to an "annual" hearing and without delay before any "other" hearing.
14. In the case of an "initial" hearing held pursuant to subsections 672.47(1) and 672.47(3) of the *Criminal Code*, where an accused is not detained at or reporting to a hospital, and a party will be advocating that the accused report to a hospital, notice of that fact shall be sent to the Review Board and the prospective receiving hospital if one is identified.

Unfit Accused

15. Where an unfit accused appears before the Review Board two years or more after the verdict of unfit to stand trial, the Crown shall inform the Review Board as to whether or not the accused has been returned to court for a determination as to whether sufficient evidence can be adduced at the time to put the accused on trial.

Expert Evidence, Documents and Authorities to be relied upon

16. Any party intending to rely upon decisions of any court or of the Review Board or any other tribunal, shall provide to every other party any such cases or decisions regardless of whether they are reported.
17. Any party intending to introduce other documentary material before the Review Board, not referred to in Rule 16, shall provide a copy of that material to the Review Board no less than 15 working days prior to the commencement of an annual hearing or as soon as practicable following receipt of the hospital report.
18. Where a party intends to rely upon written material that is greater than 25 pages in length it shall provide 8 copies to the Review Board 15 days prior to an annual hearing and as soon as practicable prior to any other hearing.
19. Hospital reports should be received by the Review Board three weeks prior to an annual hearing and, where applicable, as soon as practicable prior to any other hearing. Where the report is, of necessity, provided within the second week prior to an annual hearing eight copies should be sent to the Review Board for distribution. Updates arising within one week prior to an annual hearing should be provided orally at the hearing.
20. Any party intending to rely upon the evidence of an expert witness, apart from the staff of the hospital or other facility at which the accused is detained or to which he or she reports, shall serve notice of this intention upon the other parties to the hearing, and to the Review Board. Notice shall be served, in the case of an annual hearing, no later than 15 working days prior to the date scheduled for the hearing or as soon practicable after receipt of the hospital report. Notice shall be served as soon as practicable prior to any other hearing.
21. Any party wishing to examine or cross-examine the author of a report or disposition information must take all available steps to ensure that the witness will be present at the hearing

Review Board Files

22. Any party or counsel for a party, may, upon application to the Chairperson, attend at the offices of the Review Board to examine an accused's file and have copies made at their expense.

Where it is not practical for a party or counsel to attend the offices of the Review Board to examine an accused's file, application may be made to the Chairperson for a list of the documents contained in the file to be provided to the party and for copies to be made and sent to the party or counsel at the expense of the requesting party.

Counsel

23. For the purpose of initial hearings held pursuant to s.672.47, the Review Board shall consider counsel of record on the information or indictment to be counsel for the accused before the Review Board.
24. Counsel should, if not retained by the accused for the hearing mentioned in the Notice of Hearing, without delay, advise the Review Board of this fact, in writing. Counsel should indicate to the Review Board as soon as practicable whether s/he will seek to be appointed as counsel for the accused.
25. In the case of an accused not represented by counsel, the Notice of Hearing shall advise the accused of his or her right to apply under the Ontario Legal Aid Plan for funding to obtain counsel.
26. Where the Review Board does not receive confirmation that an accused (who is reporting to or detained in a hospital) has retained counsel, the Review Board shall notify the Area Director of the Ontario Legal Aid Plan and the Patient Advocate of the Psychiatric Patient Advocate Office at the relevant hospital four weeks prior to an "annual" hearing and seven working days prior to any "other" hearing in order to ensure that the accused is apprised of his right to counsel and Legal Aid.
27. It is mandatory that an accused be represented by counsel where the accused is unfit to stand trial or whenever interests of justice so require. Where such an accused has not been granted legal aid, counsel should notify the Review Board so that the issue of the appointment of counsel may be considered prior to the time of the hearing.

Lengthy Hearings

28. If counsel for a party has reasonable grounds to believe the hearing related to the accused will take more than two hours or will be unusually complex, counsel shall advise the Review Board as soon as practicable.

Pre-hearing Conferences

29. Where the Review Board receives notice that a hearing is expected to take longer than two hours or that the hearing may be unusually complex, the Review Board may request the parties to participate in a pre-hearing conference to in order to determine the issues and the appropriate amount of time required for the hearing.

Rescheduling of Hearings

30. Where a party has obtained the written consent of all other parties, and the rescheduling is one which may be lawfully granted, the Chairperson may reschedule a hearing.

Early Reviews

31. Where a hospital requests an early review an up-dated hospital report should be received prior to the hearing.

Adjournment Requests

32. Where a party requests an adjournment of a hearing or motion and all parties do not consent to the adjournment, the issue shall be considered and determined by the Review Board at the outset of the scheduled hearing.
33. Any party seeking an adjournment shall serve every other party with a Notice of Motion and file a Notice of Motion with the Review Board, along with any materials in support, not less than three weeks prior to an "annual" hearing and without delay prior to any other hearing. Where a hospital report is received by the parties less than15 days prior to the scheduled date of an annual hearing, the Notice of Motion for adjournment shall be served and filed as soon as practicable following receipt of the hospital report.

Witness Fees

34. The Review Board is not responsible for the payment of any costs, witness fees, or disbursements which may arise from the preparation of any report or attendance at hearings before the Review Board.

Dispositions and Reasons

35. The registrar shall issue Dispositions and Reasons as two separate documents.

Appeals

36. Where counsel for a party appeals against a Disposition of the Review Board a copy of the Notice of Appeal shall be served upon the Review Board.

The Honourable Douglas H. Carruthers, Q.C., Chairperson
Ontario Review Board

APPENDIX C

Criminal Code Forms

FORM 48: ASSESSMENT ORDER OF THE COURT

This form is contained in the *Criminal Code*. It has been modified slightly in order to permit the administrator of the hospital to return the accused to court earlier than anticipated if the assessment is complete prior to the return date on the information.

When an accused is to be returned to court earlier than anticipated, the administrator issues a letter which authorizes the wagon to pick up the accused and take the accused to court. The administrator contacts the court clerk at courtroom 102, who adds the information to the list. Duty counsel will notify counsel if the accused has retained counsel or, alternatively, take instructions.

FORM 48
(Section 672.13)
ASSESSMENT ORDER OF THE COURT

Canada,
Province of
(*territorial division*)

Whereas I have reasonable grounds to believe that evidence of the mental condition of (*name of accused*), who has been charged with ________, may be necessary to determine*

- □ whether the accused is unfit to stand trial
- □ whether the accused suffered from a mental disorder so as to exempt the accused from criminal responsibility by virtue of subsection 16(1) of the *Criminal Code* at the time of the act or omission charged against the accused
- □ whether the balance of the mind of the accused was disturbed at the time of commission of the alleged offence, if the accused is a female person charged with an offence arising out of the death of her newly-born child
- □ if a verdict of unfit to stand trial or a verdict of not criminally responsible on account of mental disorder has been rendered in respect of the accused, the appropriate disposition to be made in respect of the accused pursuant to section 672.54 or 672.58 of the Criminal Code
- □ if a verdict of unfit to stand trial has been rendered in respect of the accused, whether the court should order a stay of proceedings under section 672.851 of the *Criminal Code*

I hereby order an assessment of the mental condition of (*name of accused*) to be conducted by/at (*name of person or service by whom or place where assessment is to be made*) for a period of ____ days.

This order is to be in force for a total of ____ days, including travelling time, during which time the accused is to remain*

- □ in custody at (place where accused is to be detained)
- □ out of custody, on the following conditions:
- □ (*set out conditions, if applicable*)

* Check applicable option.

Dated this _____ day of ___________ a.d. ______, at _________.

____

(Signature of justice or judge or clerk of the court, as the case may be)

FORM 48.1: ASSESSMENT ORDER OF THE REVIEW BOARD

This form is contained in the *Criminal Code*. It appeared for the first time with the proclamation of Bill C-10. It may be used by the Review Board to order the assessment of the accused pursuant to the provisions of section 672.121 of the *Criminal Code*.

FORM 48.1
(Section 672.13)
ASSESSMENT ORDER OF THE REVIEW BOARD

Canada,
Province of
(*territorial division*)

Whereas I have reasonable grounds to believe that evidence of the mental condition of (*name of accused*), who has been charged with ______, may be necessary to*

- □ if a verdict of unfit to stand trial or a verdict of not criminally responsible on account of mental disorder has been rendered in respect of the accused, make a disposition under section 672.54 of the *Criminal Code*
- □ if a verdict of unfit to stand trial has been rendered in respect of the accused, determine whether the Review Board should make a recommendation to the court that has jurisdiction in respect of the offence charged against the accused to hold an inquiry to determine whether a stay of proceedings should be ordered in accordance with section 672.851 of the *Criminal Code*

I hereby order an assessment of the mental condition of (*name of accused*) to be conducted by/at (*name of person or service by whom or place where assessment is to be made*) for a period of ________ days.

This order is to be in force for a total of ________ days, including travelling time, during which time the accused is to remain*

- □ in custody at (*place where accused is to be detained*)
- □ out of custody, on the following conditions:
- □ (*set out conditions, if applicable*)

* Check applicable option.

Dated this ________ day of ________________ a.d. ____, at ________ .

____

(Signature of Chairperson of the Review Board)

TREATMENT ORDER (SECTION 672.58)

This form is not contained in the *Criminal Code*. The following form is a creation of one of this book's authors. It is a modified version of a form produced by the Ontario Ministry of the Attorney General. It has been modified slightly in order to permit the administrator of the hospital to return the accused to court earlier than anticipated if the treatment has been successful, and the accused rendered fit, prior to the return date on the information.

When an accused is to be returned to court earlier than anticipated, the administrator issues a letter which authorizes the delivery of the accused back to court. The administrator contacts the court clerk, who adds the information to the list. Duty counsel will notify counsel if the accused has retained counsel or, alternatively, take instructions.

TREATMENT ORDER

Ontario Court of Justice

CANADA *Section 672.58*
PROVINCE OF ONTARIO
Toronto (Region)

WHEREAS (hereinafter referred to as the "Accused") (*name of accused*) has been charged with the following offence(s) (*charges*)

AND WHEREAS the accused was found unfit to stand trial on (*today's date*) by (*name of Judge or Justice*)

AND WHEREAS the prosecutor has applied for a treatment order pursuant to section 672.58 of the *Criminal Code*

AND WHEREAS the Court is satisfied on the basis of testimony of a medical practitioner that:

i) a specified treatment should be administered to the accused for the purpose of making the accused fit to stand trial within a period not to exceed 60 days;
ii) without the treatment the accused is likely to remain unfit to stand trial;
iii) the risk of harm to the accused from the treatment is not disproportionate to the benefit anticipated to be derived; and
iv) the treatment is the least restrictive and least intrusive that could be provided for the purpose.

AND WHEREAS the following person or persons have given their consent as required by s. 672.62:

- ☐ ____________________ the person in charge of the hospital where the accused is to be treated or
- ☐ ____________________ the person to whom responsibility for the treatment of the accused has been assigned by the court.

I HEREBY DIRECT the treatment of the accused is to be conducted by/at (*name of person or service by whom or place where treatment is to be administered*) for a period of _____ days (*Not to exceed 60 days*)

I HEREBY DIRECT that the specific treatment to be administered to the accused be as follows:

I HEREBY DIRECT that during the time of the treatment the accused is to remain:
(Check applicable option)

- ☐ in custody at ______________ and shall return to 102 court (*place where accused to be detained*) on _________ at ___________ or such earlier date specified by the Administrator of the hospital. (*return date*) (*time*)
- ☐ out of custody, on the following conditions: (*set out conditions, where applicable*)

Dated at the *City of Toronto* this ______________________ (today's date)

____

(Signature of judge or justice as the case may be)

"KEEP FIT" ORDER (SECTION 672.29)

This form is not contained in the *Criminal Code*. It is the creation of one of this book's authors. It covers the provisions of section 672.29 of the *Criminal Code*, which allow for an accused who obtains a verdict of "fit to stand trial" to be hospitalized until the completion of his trial in order to preserve fitness. It is to be used to preserve fitness *only after the issue has been tried.*

CANADA *Section 672.29*
PROVINCE OF ONTARIO
Toronto
(Region)

WARRANT OF COMMITTAL

Detention of Accused in Hospital Until Completion of Trial (672.29)

To the peace officers in the said region, and to the keeper (administrator, warden) of the (prison, hospital or other appropriate place where the accused is currently detained)

This warrant is issued for the committal of: (hereinafter called the accused) (*accused name*)

Whereas the accused has been charged that (set out briefly the offence in respect of which the accused was charged)

And whereas the accused, upon a trial of the issue, has been found *FIT TO STAND TRIAL* and there are reasonable grounds to believe that the accused would become unfit to stand trial if released.

It is therefore Ordered, pursuant to the provisions of section 672.29 of the *Criminal Code* of Canada, that you, ____________________ in His Majesty's name, take the accused in custody and convey the accused safely to the ____________________ (*hospital*) and there deliver the accused to the Administrator with the following precept:

I do therefore command you the said Administrator to receive the accused in your custody in the said hospital and to keep the accused safely there until the completion of the accused's trial or such earlier time as may be Ordered.

Dated at the ____________________ (*City*) this ____________________ (today's date)

____

(Signature of judge or justice as the case may be)

HOSPITAL PENDING REVIEW BOARD (SECTION 672.46(2))

This form is not contained in the *Criminal Code*. It is the creation of one of this book's authors. The following form covers the provisions of subsection 672.46(2) of the *Criminal Code*, which permit the court to place an accused, upon the verdict of either unfit or NCR, in hospital pending the accused's hearing before the Review Board, rather than returning the accused to jail.

CANADA *Section 672.46(2)*
PROVINCE OF ONTARIO
Toronto
(Region)

WARRANT OF COMMITTAL
Detention of Accused in Hospital Pending Disposition of the Ontario Review Board (672.46(2))

To the peace officers in the said region, and to the keeper (administrator, warden) of the (*prison, hospital or other appropriate place where the accused is currently detained*)

This warrant is issued for the committal of: (hereinafter called the accused) (*accused name*)

Whereas the accused has been charged that (*set out briefly the offence in respect of which the accused was charged*)

And whereas the accused, upon a trial of the issue, has been found

Check One

- ◻ UNFIT TO STAND TRIAL
- ◻ NOT CRIMINALLY RESPONSIBLE ON ACCOUNT OF MENTAL DISORDER, and a Disposition has not been held pursuant to the provisions of section 672.54,

It is therefore Ordered, pursuant to the provisions of section 672.46(2) of the *Criminal Code* of Canada, that you, in His Majesty's name, take the accused in custody and convey the accused safely to the (*hospital*) and there deliver the accused to the Administrator with the following precept:

I do therefore command you the said Administrator to receive the accused in your custody in the said hospital and to keep the accused safely there until a hearing has been held by the Ontario Review Board and a Disposition made.

Dated at the ______________________ (*City*) this ______________________ (today's date)

____

(Signature of judge or justice as the case may be)

DISPOSITION: DETENTION IN HOSPITAL (SECTION 672.54(C))

Form 49

This form is contained in the *Criminal Code*. It is used where the court makes a disposition (for either an unfit or an NCR) pursuant to the provisions of section 672.54(c). This form, along with a "New Accused Information Sheet" filled out by the Crown, is sent to the Review Board within forty-eight hours. Note that any disposition of the court (other than section 672.54(a)) is reviewed by the Review Board within ninety days.

FORM 49
(Section 672.57)
WARRANT OF COMMITTAL
DISPOSITION OF DETENTION

Canada,
Province of
(*territorial division*)

To the peace officers in the said (*territorial division*) and to the keeper (*administrator, warden*) of the (*prison, hospital or other appropriate place where the accused is detained*).

This warrant is issued for the committal of _____, of ___________, (*occupation*), hereinafter called the accused.

Whereas the accused has been charged that (*set out briefly the offence in respect of which the accused was charged*);

And whereas the accused was found*

- □ unfit to stand trial
- □ not criminally responsible on account of mental disorder

This is, therefore, to command you, in His Majesty's name, to take the accused in custody and convey the accused safely to the (*prison, hospital or other appropriate place*) at _______, and there deliver the accused to the keeper (administrator, warden) with the following precept:

I do therefore command you the said keeper (administrator, warden) to receive the accused in your custody in the said (*prison, hospital or other appropriate place*) and to keep the accused safely there until the accused is delivered by due course of law.

The following are the conditions to which the accused shall be subject while in your (*prison, hospital or other appropriate place*):

The following are the powers regarding the restrictions (*and the limits and conditions on those restrictions*) on the liberty of the accused that are hereby delegated to you the said keeper (administrator, warden) of the said (*prison, hospital or other appropriate place*):

* Check applicable option.

Dated this ____ day of __________ a.d. _______, at ________.

____

(Signature of judge, clerk of the court, provincial court judge or chairperson of the Review Board)

DISPOSITION: DISCHARGE SUBJECT TO CONDITIONS (SECTION 672.54(B))

Disposition

This form is not contained in the *Criminal Code*. It is the creation of one of this book's authors. Parliament did not include a form for the making of a disposition where the disposition is not a custodial one. Where the accused is to be discharged absolutely (section 672.54(a)), no form is required; however, where the accused is to be discharged subject to conditions (section 672.54(b)), the following form may be used to record the disposition.

CANADA *Section 672.54(b)*
PROVINCE OF ONTARIO
Toronto
(Region)

DISPOSITION

Accused Out of Custody

WHEREAS (hereinafter referred to as the "Accused") (*name of accused*) has been charged with (*set out briefly the offence in respect of which the accused was charged*)

And whereas the accused, upon a trial of the issue, has been found

Check One

- ◻ UNFIT TO STAND TRIAL
- ◻ NOT CRIMINALLY RESPONSIBLE ON ACCOUNT OF MENTAL DISORDER,

and a hearing has taken place pursuant to the provisions of section 672.47(1) of the *Criminal Code* of Canada and it has been determined that the least onerous and least restrictive Disposition is that the accused be discharged subject to conditions, it is Ordered that: [*list terms of Discharge*]

THIS IS THEREFORE TO COMMAND you, ______________________, in His Majesty's name, to comply with the terms of this Disposition and, upon Notice, to appear before the Ontario Review Board as directed.

Dated at the City of ____________________ this ____________________ (today's date)

____

(Signature of judge or justice as the case may be)

HOSPITAL ASSESSMENT: OUT OF CUSTODY

Form 6: Assessment by a Hospital of an Accused who is Out of Custody[1]

This form reflects the provisions of subsection 21(1) of the *Mental Health Act* of Ontario. These provisions allow for the assessment of an accused who appears before the court out of custody. Note that a precondition to the making of the order is the consent of the prospective assessing facility.

Form 6

Mental Health Act

Order for Attendance for Examination
Subsection 21(1) of the Act

In the (*name of court*) held at (*address*)

TO (*name of psychiatric facility*)

WHEREAS (*name of person in full*) (*address*)

Strike out inapplicable words	is charged with	(*offence*)
	has been convicted of	

AND WHEREAS he/she has appeared before me and I have reason to believe that he/she suffers from mental disorder;

AND WHEREAS I have ascertained from (*name of senior physician, as defined in the Act*) the senior physician of (*name of psychiatric facility*) that the services of the said psychiatric facility are available to the above-named person;

I HEREBY ORDER that the above-named person attend, by appointment, the said psychiatric facility for examination;

____________________ (Judge)

Date ____________________ (day/month/year)

1 *Mental Health Act*, R.R.O. 1990, Reg. 741, Form 6.

HOSPITAL ASSESSMENT: IN CUSTODY

Form 8: Assessment by A Hospital of an Accused Who is in Custody[2]

This form reflects the provisions of subsection 22(1) of the *Mental Health Act* of Ontario. These provisions allow for the assessment of an accused who appears before the court in custody. Note that a precondition to the making of the order is the consent of the prospective assessing facility.

FORM 8
Mental Health Act

ORDER FOR ADMISSION
Subsection 22(1) of the Act

In the (*name of court*) held at (*address*)

TO the Peace Officers in the ____________________ of ____________________

AND TO (*name of psychiatric facility*)

WHEREAS (*name of person in full*) (*address*) is a person charged with (*offence*) contrary to section ____ of the ____________________;

AND WHEREAS he/she has appeared before me and I have reason to believe that he/she suffers from mental disorder;

AND WHEREAS I have ascertained from (*name of senior physician, as defined in the Act*) the senior physician of (*name of psychiatric facility*) that the services of the said psychiatric facility are available to the above-named person;

I HEREBY ORDER that the above-named shall be remanded for admission as a patient to the said psychiatric facility for a period of not more than ____________________;

AND I FURTHER ORDER and direct you, the said Peace Officers, or any of you, to convey him/her to said psychiatric facility;

AND I AUTHORIZE you, the authorities of said psychiatric facility, to admit him/her in accordance with this order.

____________________ (Judge)

Date ____________________ (day / month / year)

2 *Mental Health Act*, R.R.O. 1990, Reg. 741, Form 8.